A TASTE OF
FRANCE

A TASTE OF
FRANCE

Regional French Cuisine

GABRIEL GATÉ

ILLUSTRATED BY ANTONIA PESENTI

hardie grant books
MELBOURNE · LONDON

TABLE OF CONTENTS

❧

Brest

BRITTANY

QuimpER

LoRier

This edition published in 2013
First published as *Taste Le Tour* in 2010

An SBS book

Hardie Grant Books (Australia)
Ground Floor, Building 1
658 Church Street
Richmond, Victoria 3121
www.hardiegrant.com.au

Hardie Grant Books (UK)
Dudley House, North Suite
34–35 Southampton Street
London WC2E 7HF
www.hardiegrant.co.uk

Copyright recipes © SBS 2010
Copyright text © Gabriel Gaté
Copyright illustrations © Antonia Pesenti

Cataloguing-in-Publication data is available from the National Library
of Australia.

ISBN 978 1 7427 0490 6

Cover and text design by Michelle Mackintosh
Colour reproduction by Splitting Image Colour Studio
Printed and bound in China by C&C Offset Printing

10 9 8 7 6 5 4 3 2 1

INTRODUCTION

✤

This cookbook is a collection of delicious regional French dishes. The recipes come from a handful of French chefs, in particular, Philippe Mouchel and myself, but also from local French pastry cooks and food artisans. Many of the dishes are easy to prepare, while others will challenge you.

I travel to France every year to produce and present a television segment featuring the best of French gastronomy. It showcases the food, wine, cheese and special dishes of all the French regions.

Discover the regions of France – steeped in history – and delight in the dishes from the orchards, vineyards, pastures, grand homes, villages and much more.

Bon appétit!

CHAPTER ONE

❧

SOUPS, STARTERS
& VEGETABLES

YOUNG VEGETABLE SOUP

Potage aux primeurs
From Paris – Ile de France

❧

*The French adore soup and this sort of vegetable potage is extremely popular
in the countryside surrounding Paris, where many vegetables for the
Parisian market are grown.*

2 medium leeks
at least 1 cup celery leaves
   or 2 celery stalks
½ cos (romaine) lettuce
1½ litres (51 fl oz/6 cups)
   chicken stock
150 g (5½ oz) peas

2 tablespoons olive oil
20 g (¾ oz) butter
2 slices bread, cut into 2.5 cm
   (1 in) cubes
4 egg yolks
salt
freshly ground black pepper

Trim and wash the leeks and cut them into thin julienne strips, about 5 cm
(2 in) long.

Shred the celery leaves (or thinly slice the stalks, if using). Wash and shred the
lettuce leaves.

In a large saucepan, bring the chicken stock to the boil. Add the leeks, celery
leaves, lettuce and peas and cook at a low boil for about 15 minutes, or until the
vegetables are soft.

Meanwhile, heat the oil and butter in a frying pan and fry the bread cubes until
lightly browned.

Place the egg yolks in a mixing bowl and whisk to combine. Slowly pour
in about 250 ml (8½ fl oz/1 cup) of hot liquid from the soup, whisking
continuously. Season with salt and pepper.

Take the soup off the heat, gradually whisk in the egg mixture, then season to
taste. Ladle into deep soup bowls and serve the croutons separately.

Serves 4–6

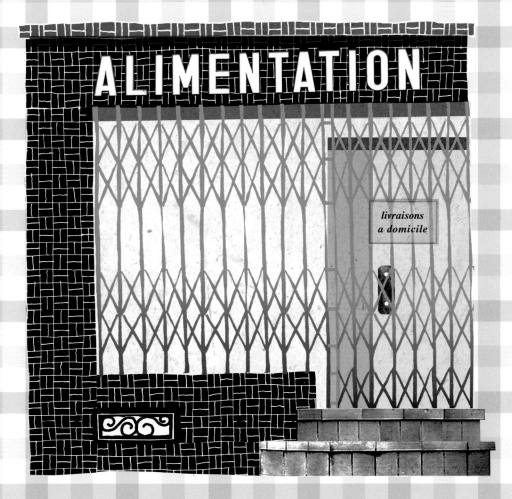

MUSSEL AND SAFFRON SOUP

Soupe de moules au saffran

From the Languedoc Region by Philippe Mouchel

❧

The French Mediterranean coast in the Languedoc region is dotted with wonderful little fishing villages where you can enjoy hearty but delicately flavoured seafood soups and stews in the local restaurants.

1 kg (2 lb) large very fresh mussels, scrubbed and beards removed
2 French shallots, thinly sliced
½ medium onion, thinly sliced
1 sprig thyme
1 bay leaf
a few parsley stalks
2 strips orange peel
250 ml (8½ fl oz/1 cup) dry white wine

3 tomatoes, peeled, seeded and diced
1 tablespoon cornflour (cornstarch)
2 tablespoons water
125 ml (4½ fl oz/½ cup) pouring cream
a good pinch of saffron threads
30 g (1 oz) butter, cubed
freshly ground black pepper
4 tablespoons finely snipped chives

Put the mussels in a large saucepan and add the shallots and onion. Tie the thyme, bay leaf, parsley stalks and orange peel together with kitchen string and add to the pot. Pour in the wine and cover with a lid. Bring to the boil over high heat and cook for a few minutes until the mussels have just opened.

Lift the mussels out of the cooking liquid into a bowl. Discard the onions and the herb bouquet. Taste the liquid and if it is too salty add a little water. Add the tomatoes and simmer for about 5 minutes. Meanwhile, remove the mussel meat from the shells and keep warm.

Mix the cornflour with the water then whisk into the simmering soup. Bring to the boil, add the cream and cook gently for a few minutes. Add the saffron then blend until smooth. Stir in the butter until melted then add plenty of pepper.

Divide the mussels among four bowls, pour on the soup and sprinkle with chives.

Serves 4

MUSSELS COOKED WITH WHITE WINE AND HERBS

Moules marinières

From the Atlantic-Poitou Region by Philippe Mouchel

❧

A survey done a few years ago showed that the average French person's favourite dish was moules marinières. The French consider it an affordable festive dish to be enjoyed on the terrace of a seaside restaurant during the long days of summer.

2 tablespoons olive oil
2 French shallots, thinly sliced
1.5 kg (3 lb) mussels, thoroughly
    scrubbed and beards removed
100 ml (3½ fl oz) dry white wine
a few sprigs parsley, plus
    2 tablespoons chopped parsley

1 bay leaf
2 sprigs thyme
freshly ground black pepper
55 g (2 oz) butter, cut into
    small pieces

Heat the oil in a large saucepan over a gentle heat. Add the shallots and cook, stirring continuously, for a few minutes. Add the mussels, white wine, parsley sprigs, bay leaf and thyme, and season with pepper. Cover with a lid and steam the mussels for about 5 minutes, until they have all opened. Shake the pan a couple of times during the cooking.

Lift the mussels out of the pan into a large serving bowl. Bring the mussel juices to the boil and boil for 2 minutes. Add the butter and stir until melted. Stir in the chopped parsley, pour the liquid over the mussels and serve at once.

Serves 2–3

FISH STEW

Bouillabaisse

From the Provence Region

❖

This fish stew specialty of Marseille is traditionally made with a selection of rock fish. When well made it is one of my favourite French dishes. It is traditionally served with fried slices of baguette and a garlic mayonnaise.

2 tablespoons extra-virgin olive oil

1 medium onion, chopped

10 cumin seeds

20 fennel seeds

1 small red chilli, thinly sliced

1 bulb fennel, cut into 8 wedges

1 kg (2 lb 3 oz) tomatoes, peeled, seeded and chopped

1 litre (34 fl oz/4 cups) fish stock

salt

freshly ground black pepper

a large pinch of saffron threads

2 kg (4 lb 6 oz) firm white fish, cleaned and heads removed

16 prawns (shrimp), shelled and deveined

16 new potatoes, peeled and cooked

2 cloves garlic, chopped

Gently heat the oil in a casserole dish. Add the onion, cumin seeds, fennel seeds and chilli and fry for 1 minute. Add the fennel wedges and fry for 1 minute. Add the tomatoes and stir for 1 minute. Add the fish stock and season with salt, pepper and saffron. Bring to the boil, then boil for 10 minutes.

Add the whole fish to the casserole dish and simmer for 10 minutes. Add the prawns and simmer for a further 5 minutes.

Transfer the fish and vegetables to a platter and garnish with boiled potatoes.

Stir the garlic into the cooking liquid and transfer to a soup tureen.

Diners serve themselves by placing the seafood and potato into deep soup plates and ladling the liquid over the top.

Serves 8

Note: French people love fish, and to obtain the maximum flavour, they always cook fish on the bone when making bouillabaisse. Then as they eat it, they patiently remove the bones from the flesh.

MARINATED SARDINES

Sardines à l'escabèche
From the Provence Region

❧

*This traditional dish of sardines, marinated with vinegar, oil and herbs,
is often associated with the historic Mediterranean Provençal city of Marseille.
Marseille is famous for its daily fish market where sardines and other seafood
are sold just hours after the catch.*

12 fresh medium sardines
3 tablespoons lemon olive oil,
    plus a little extra for drizzling
salt
freshly ground black pepper
½ medium onion, very thinly sliced
1 medium baby carrot, thinly sliced
1 teaspoon coriander seeds

1 bay leaf
4 sprigs thyme
2 cloves garlic, unpeeled
60 ml (2 fl oz/¼ cup) good-
    quality white vinegar (I use
    Champagne vinegar)
125 ml (4½ fl oz/½ cup)
    cold water

Clean the insides of the sardines, scale them and cut off the heads. Dry the
sardines with paper towel.

Heat 2 tablespoons of the oil in a large frying pan and fry the sardines for
1–2 minutes on each side. Be careful not to overcook them. Season the sardines
with salt and pepper and arrange them on a flat platter.

Heat the remaining oil in a separate frying pan. Add the onion, carrot, coriander
seeds, bay leaf, thyme and garlic cloves and cook gently for 2 minutes. Add the
vinegar and water, bring to the boil and simmer for 15 minutes.

Spoon the hot liquid, herbs and vegetables over the sardines. Allow to cool,
cover with plastic wrap and refrigerate for 24 hours. The sardines will absorb
the liquid.

Just before serving, drizzle the sardines with a little extra lemon olive oil.

Serves 4 as a starter

CRAYFISH AND POTATO SALAD

Salade de langouste aux pommes de terre

From the Atlantic Island Region by Philippe Mouchel

❖

The Atlantic coast south of the Loire River is dotted with many islands, one of which is Noirmoutier, which is famous for its shellfish and new-season potatoes. As a boy I enjoyed several summer holidays in Noirmoutier.

1 x 800 g (1 lb 12 oz) cooked crayfish

2–4 small new potatoes, cooked in their skins

125 g (4 oz) green beans, cooked but firm

2 tomatoes, peeled, quartered and seeded

a few green salad leaves

juice of 1 lemon

sea salt

freshly ground black pepper

4 tablespoons olive oil

2 tablespoons finely snipped chives

fresh herbs, to serve (optional)

Remove the crayfish from the shell and cut the tail meat into slices just less than 1 cm (½ in) thick.

Peel and slice the potatoes.

Arrange the crayfish and potato slices attractively on two plates. Garnish with a little bouquet of green beans and four tomato quarters. Top with salad leaves.

To make the dressing, whisk the lemon juice with a little salt and pepper then whisk in the olive oil. Add the chives and drizzle the dressing over the salad.

Garnish with extra fresh herbs if you wish, then serve.

Serves 2

CRAYFISH À LA PARISIENNE

Langouste à la Parisienne
From the Paris Region by Philippe Mouchel

❧

During my younger days I worked in a wonderful Parisian seafood restaurant called Prunier where I learned to prepare this classic dish of crayfish with a diced vegetable and mayonnaise salad. This is Philippe's recipe and to present the dish he uses 10 cm (4 in) PVC rings.

3 tablespoons diced turnips,
　about 6 mm (¼ in) square
3 tablespoons diced carrots,
　about 6 mm (¼ in) square
3 tablespoons diced beans,
　about 6 mm (¼ in) square
3 tablespoons diced potatoes,
　about 6 mm (¼ in) square
2 tablespoons peas
1 egg yolk
2 tablespoons mustard

salt
freshly ground black pepper
2 teaspoons vinegar
100 ml (3½ fl oz) olive oil,
　plus a little extra for drizzling
1 x 400 g (14 oz) cooked
　crayfish
a few cos (romaine) lettuce
　leaves
a few chives, to garnish

Cook the turnips, carrots, beans, potatoes and peas separately in boiling salted water until tender (either use separate saucepans or change the water for each vegetable). Drain each vegetable well then place on a clean cloth to absorb excess water.

In a bowl, mix the egg yolk with the mustard, a little salt and pepper and the vinegar. Gradually pour in the oil, whisking continuously, until you obtain a thick mayonnaise.

Place the cooked, drained vegetables in a bowl and mix in half the mayonnaise.

Remove the crayfish tail meat and cut it into 1 cm (½ in) slices.

To serve, place a PVC ring in the centre of each plate. Spoon in one-third of the vegetable mixture and flatten the surface with a spoon. Arrange a few overlapping slices of crayfish on top of the vegetables and carefully remove the PVC rings. Top with a few lettuce leaves and a small dollop of mayonnaise.

Drizzle on a little extra oil, sprinkle with a few chives and serve.

Serves 3

COUNTRY-STYLE PÂTÉ WITH PISTACHIOS

Pâté de campagne à la pistache

From the Burgundy Region by Stéphane Langlois

❧

Burgundy is one of the great gastronomic regions of France, with its superb wines and meat – including the charcuterie (smallgoods), such as this festive country-style paté which used to be made on the farm and served for special occasions.

750 g (1 lb 10 oz) lean pork leg meat, cubed
350 g (12 oz) pork fat, cubed
550 g (1 lb 4 oz) chicken livers, cleaned and trimmed
a handful of parsley leaves
½ brown onion, roughly chopped
40 g (1½ oz) salt (or less, to taste)
1 teaspoon ground white pepper
1 teaspoon mixed (pumpkin pie) spice
1 tablespoon chopped garlic

2 teaspoons dried thyme
60 ml (2 fl oz/¼ cup) cognac or brandy
2 tablespoons cornflour (cornstarch)
2 medium eggs
120 g (4 oz) shelled pistachios
a few strips of thinly cut pork fat, optional
10 g (⅓ oz) powdered gelatine
300 ml (10 fl oz) warm water

Preheat the oven to 90°C (195°F). Grease a 2-litre (68-fl oz/8-cup) terrine dish.

Mix together the pork, pork fat, chicken livers, parsley and onion. Put the mixture through a mincer then transfer to a bowl and stir in the salt, white pepper, spice, garlic and dried thyme. Add the cognac, cornflour, eggs and pistachio nuts and mix everything together thoroughly.

Tip the pâté mixture into the terrine dish and smooth the top. Decorate with a few strips of the thinly cut pork fat, if you wish, arranged in a criss-cross pattern.

Place the terrine in a baking dish and pour in hot water to a depth of about 5 cm (2 in) to create a bain-marie. Bake for about 3 hours. When it is cooked, the temperature of the terrine will have reached 80°C (175°F) at its centre.

Remove the terrine from the oven and stand on a cool surface. Dissolve the gelatine in the warm water and pour over the terrine. Allow the terrine to cool, then refrigerate until ready to serve. Slice the terrine while still in the dish and serve with gherkins (pickles) and French bread.

Serves 12

POTATO GALETTES WITH A WALNUT AND ROQUEFORT CHEESE SALAD

Galettes de pomme de terre, salade de roquefort aux noix
From the Languedoc Region

❧

This dish is so French – and so typical of the northern part of Languedoc, not far from where the famous roquefort blue cheese is made. The use of duck fat to cook the potatoes is essential for the authentic flavour. It is available from specialist butchers, good delicatessens and some supermarkets.

1 clove garlic, finely chopped
salt
freshly ground pepper
1 tablespoon red wine vinegar
3 tablespoons olive oil
80 g (2¾ oz) mixed green leaves
60 g (2 oz) roquefort cheese,
  broken into small pieces

4 shelled walnuts, very
  roughly chopped
2 medium potatoes
2 tablespoons chopped parsley
2 tablespoons duck fat

Place half the garlic in a large mixing bowl with a little salt and pepper and the vinegar and whisk together well. Whisk in the oil gradually. Add the green leaves, cheese and walnuts to the bowl and toss everything together gently.

Grate the potatoes onto a plate and pat dry with paper towel. Tip into a bowl with the remaining garlic and the chopped parsley. Season with salt and pepper and mix well.

Heat the duck fat in a 20 cm (8 in) frying pan. When the fat is hot, add the potato mixture to form a large galette about 1 cm (½ in) thick. Press with the back of a spoon or fork to flatten and cook on medium heat for a few minutes. Carefully turn the galette over and cook the other side (to turn the galette, slide it onto a plate, then invert the plate and slide the galette back into the pan).

Cut the cooked galette in half or quarters and divide between two plates. Serve with the dressed salad.

Serves 2

ROSCOVITE SALAD WITH CAULIFLOWER AND PRAWNS

Salade Roscovite

From the Brittany Region by Philippe Mouchel

❖

This classic Breton salad was named after the coastal town of Roscoff in Brittany. The locals adore cauliflower, which is just as important as the prawns (shrimp) in this lovely salad. For an elegant presentation, use 10 cm (4 in) PVC rings.

¼ cauliflower, cut into medium florets
12 cm (5 in) piece of cucumber, cut into cubes
2 potatoes, cooked in their skins and cubed
1 egg yolk
1 teaspoon dijon mustard
salt
freshly ground pepper

1 lemon
125 ml (4½ fl oz/½ cup) extra-virgin olive oil, plus 2 tablespoons extra
3 tablespoons pouring cream
3 tablespoons chervil leaves
3 tablespoons tarragon leaves
16 cooked prawns (shrimp), peeled and deveined
4 hard-boiled eggs, quartered

Cook the cauliflower florets in boiling salted water for a few minutes, until just tender. Drain and cool in cold water. Drain again and cut into smaller pieces.

Place the cauliflower, cucumber and potato in a bowl.

In a second bowl make a mayonnaise by whisking the egg yolk with the mustard, a little salt and pepper and a few drops of lemon juice. Slowly drizzle in 125 ml (4½ fl oz/½ cup) oil, whisking continuously until thick and creamy. Whisk in the cream and set aside.

Roughly chop two-thirds of the chervil and tarragon leaves, reserving the rest for garnish. Add to the vegetables and toss with the extra 2 tablespoons of oil.

Carefully spread 2 tablespoons of the creamy mayonnaise over each of four plates. Place a PVC ring in the centre and spoon a few tablespoons of the vegetable salad into the rings. Lift the ring away carefully.

Divide the prawns and hard-boiled eggs among the plates, arranging them attractively around the vegetable salad. Scatter with the reserved chervil and tarragon on top and serve.

Serves 4

ASPARAGUS AND GOAT'S CHEESE TART

Tarte aux asperges et au fromage de chèvre
From the Loire Valley Region by Philippe Mouchel

❧

*The sandy soil of the Loire Valley produces superb asparagus,
and almost every restaurant in the region serves an asparagus dish in the two
or three months leading up to the Tour de France.*

400 g (14 oz) rolled puff pastry
2 egg yolks
1 teaspoon water
16 thin green asparagus spears,
 trimmed

2 tablespoons pouring cream
salt
freshly ground pepper
85 g (3 oz) fresh goat's cheese

Preheat the oven to 170°C (325°F). Line a baking tray with baking (parchment) paper.

Cut the pastry into a rectangle about 10 x 30 cm (4 x 12 in) and place on the baking tray. Using the blade of a knife, lightly mark a 1 cm (½ in) border down both long sides of the pastry. Weight down the centre of the pastry (use baking paper with rice or small pastry weights) to stop it from rising when baked.

Lightly beat one of the egg yolks with the water and use to brush along the pastry edges. Bake for 15–20 minutes, or until the edges have risen and are golden brown.

Drop the asparagus spears into lightly salted boiling water for 2–3 minutes, then drain well.

Remove the baking paper and weights from the pastry. Lightly beat the remaining egg yolk with the cream and brush over the centre of the pastry. Season with salt and pepper. Top neatly with the cooked asparagus and spoon any remaining egg yolk and cream over the top. Dot with small pieces of goat's cheese and season with a little more salt and pepper. Return to the oven and bake for about 5 minutes, until the cheese is warm and lightly browned. Cut in half before serving.

Serves 2

YABBIES IN PUFF PASTRY

Ecrevisses en chausson

From the Alps Region by Philippe Mouchel

❧

Yabbies are very popular in France and are found on the menus
of the best French restaurants, especially around the Alps region
where there are lots of freshwater streams.

2 rectangles rolled puff pastry,
   8 x 12 cm x 3 mm thick
   (3 x 4 in x ⅛ in thick)
1 egg yolk
2 teaspoons cold water
6 cm (2½ in) piece carrot
6 cm (2½ in) piece leek
6 cm (2½ in) piece celery
1 teaspoon olive oil
40 g (1½ oz) butter

2 tablespoons pouring cream
½ tablespoon finely
   chopped tarragon
½ tablespoon finely
   chopped parsley
6 thin slices truffle
12 cooked yabbies, shelled
salt
freshly ground black pepper

Preheat the oven to 180°C (350°F). Line a baking tray with baking (parchment) paper. Place the puff pastry rectangles on the prepared baking tray. Using the tip of a knife, lightly mark a smaller rectangle inside each pastry rectangle, forming a 5 mm (¼ in) border.

Mix the egg yolk and water together and brush over the pastry. Bake for 15–18 minutes, or until lightly browned and risen. It should rise at least 2 cm (¾ in) if the pastry is good quality.

Thinly slice the carrot, leek and celery, then cut into thin julienne strips. Heat the oil and butter in a small saucepan over medium heat. Add the vegetables and cook for a few minutes until soft. Add the cream, tarragon and parsley, then add the truffle slices and yabbies and reheat. Season to taste.

Cut the smaller rectangle out of each cooked pastry rectangle and set this 'lid' aside. Remove any excess pastry from the centre to create a cavity. Divide the yabby and vegetable mixture between the pastry cases, replace the pastry lids and serve straight away.

Serves 2

GRATIN OF YABBIES

Gratin d'écrevisses

From the Alps Region by Philippe Mouchel

❧

This stunning dish used to be served in many of the top three-star restaurants all over France. It's fairly rich but is a real classic and a great dish to learn and to serve for special occasions.

1.5 kg (3 lb 5 oz) cooked yabbies (or other crayfish)
4 tablespoons olive oil
45 g (1½ oz) butter
3 French shallots, thinly sliced
1 fennel stalk
1 tablespoon tomato paste (concentrated purée)
1 tomato, diced
60 ml (2 fl oz/¼ cup) cognac
125 ml (4½ fl oz/½ cup) madeira
125 ml (4½ fl oz/½ cup) white wine, plus 2 tablespoons extra
500 ml (17 fl oz/2 cups) crayfish or fish stock

1 bay leaf
2 sprigs thyme
80 ml (2½ fl oz/⅓ cup) pouring cream
a pinch of cayenne pepper
2 egg yolks
100 g (3½ oz) warm melted butter
juice of ¼ lemon
400 g (14 oz) cooked spinach
1 clove garlic, chopped
salt
freshly ground black pepper

Detach and reserve the yabby heads from the bodies and shell the yabby tails.

Heat 2 tablespoons of the oil in a heavy, cast-iron saucepan. When very hot, add the yabby heads and stir well for a couple of minutes, pressing on the heads from time to time to extract more flavour.

Add half the butter to the pan then add the shallots and fennel and stir well. Add the tomato paste and stir well. Stir in the diced tomato, cognac, madeira and wine and bring to the boil. Add the stock, bay leaf and thyme and simmer for 20 minutes, uncovered. Stir in the cream and cayenne pepper and cook for a further 5 minutes.

Strain the yabby sauce through a chinois or very fine sieve into a saucepan, pressing on the shells to extract the maximum flavour. Simmer the sauce over medium heat until reduced to about 325 ml (11 fl oz).

Place the egg yolks and the 2 extra tablespoons of wine in a medium bowl and sit it over a saucepan of simmering water. Whisk the yolks over the heat for about 5 minutes until light and fluffy. Remove the bowl from the saucepan and gradually add the melted butter, whisking continuously to form a creamy sauce. Whisk in the lemon juice.

Melt a teaspoon of the remaining butter in a saucepan. Add the cooked spinach and garlic and warm through gently.

Melt the rest of the butter and the remaining 2 tablespoons of oil in a pan and gently reheat the yabby tails. Season to taste with salt and pepper and gently stir in the yabby sauce.

Arrange the spinach in a 25 cm (10 in) gratin dish. Top with the yabbies and sauce and place under a hot grill (broiler) until lightly browned on top. Serve immediately.

Serves 4

MUSSEL GRATIN WITH SPINACH

Moules gratinées aux épinards

From the North Coast Region by Philippe Mouchel

❦

*This mussel dish is out of this world, and so French, with the flavour
of garlic butter.*

1 tablespoon olive oil
125 g (4 oz) butter
1 French shallot, finely chopped
20 mussels in their shells,
  thoroughly scrubbed and
  beards removed
10 parsley stalks, plus
  3 tablespoons chopped parsley
60 ml (2 fl oz/¼ cup) dry
  white wine

2 cloves garlic, chopped
juice of ½ lemon
salt
freshly ground black pepper
200 g (7 oz) baby spinach leaves
60 ml (2 fl oz/¼ cup) pouring
  cream
3 tablespoons dried breadcrumbs

Heat the oil and 1 teaspoon of butter in a large saucepan. Stir in the shallot and cook for 2 minutes. Add the mussels, parsley stalks and wine to the pan. Cover with a lid and cook for a few minutes until the mussels have just opened.

Place the rest of the butter in a small bowl, keeping 1 teaspoon in reserve. Add the garlic, chopped parsley, lemon juice and a little salt and pepper.

Heat the remaining teaspoon of butter in a large saucepan and cook the spinach until wilted. Drain well.

Heat the cream in a small saucepan and when it boils, stir in the wilted spinach.

Remove the mussel meat from the shells. Arrange 20 half-shells on a large plate or serving dish. Spoon a little of the creamed spinach into each shell and top with a mussel. Spoon a little herbed butter onto each mussel, then sprinkle lightly with breadcrumbs. Place under a hot grill for a few minutes until the breadcrumbs are lightly browned. Serve immediately.

Serves 2

BUCKWHEAT PANCAKES FROM BRITTANY

Galettes Bretonnes au Sarazin

From the Brittany Region by Jean-Marie Blanchot

⚜

*These savoury buckwheat pancakes are the pride of Brittany's cuisine
and I am very fond of them myself. They're usually prepared on special circular
hotplates about 30 cm (12 in) in diameter, but at home you can use
a very large non-stick frying pan.*

250 ml (8½ fl oz/1 cup) cold water
½ teaspoon salt
200 g (7 oz) buckwheat flour
10 g (⅓ oz) salted butter, melted,
   plus extra unmelted butter

4 eggs
125 g (4 oz) grated gruyère
   cheese
4–8 thin slices of ham

Place most of the water and the salt in a large bowl and mix well. Add the flour
and whisk to a smooth batter. It should fall like a ribbon when you lift the whisk.
If necessary, add a little extra water.

Mix in the melted butter until well incorporated. Cover the batter and rest in
the fridge for about 4 hours.

When ready to cook the pancakes, lightly grease a large non-stick frying pan
with extra butter and heat over medium heat. Pour in enough batter to cover the
base very thinly. When the underside of the pancake is dry, lower the heat and
rub the surface of the pancake with a piece of extra butter.

Break an egg in the centre and spread the white all over the pancake, keeping
the yolk intact. Sprinkle with grated cheese and top with a slice or two of ham.

Using a spatula, carefully fold the sides of the pancake in towards the yolk to
form a square. Cook for an extra minute or two, then transfer to a warm plate
while you make the rest of the pancakes.

Serves 4 as a starter

CHEESE SOUFFLÉ

Soufflé au fromage
From the Jura Region

❧

The Jura mountain range bordering the Franche Compté and Switzerland produces really flavoursome cheeses with lovely melting qualities. They are used frequently by local cooks in recipes such as this delicious soufflé.

30 g (1 oz) butter
30 g (1 oz) plain
   (all-purpose) flour
350 ml (12 fl oz) milk
¼ teaspoon freshly
   grated nutmeg
a good pinch of cayenne pepper
freshly ground black pepper

2 small egg yolks
55 g (2 oz) grated gruyère
   cheese
55 g (2 oz) grated emmental
   cheese
6 egg whites
a pinch of cream of tartar

Preheat the oven to 180°C (350°F). Butter and flour an 18 cm (7 in) soufflé mould.

Melt the butter in a saucepan over medium heat. Whisk in the flour and cook for about 2 minutes. Slowly add the milk, whisking constantly until it forms a smooth white sauce. Cook gently for 3–4 minutes, then turn off the heat.

Mix in the nutmeg, cayenne pepper and a little black pepper. Add the egg yolks and grated cheese and mix in well. Transfer the soufflé base to a large bowl.

Whisk the egg whites with the cream of tartar until stiff. Mix a little of the beaten whites into the soufflé base to loosen the mixture, then gently fold in the remaining whites.

Pour the soufflé mixture into the prepared soufflé mould and smooth the surface. If you wish, you can decorate the surface with small, flat, diamond-shaped pieces of cheese for effect.

Bake for about 35 minutes, then serve immediately. Take care when carrying the hot soufflé to the table. To serve, spoon the soufflé onto warmed plates.

Serves 4 as a starter

FRENCH-STYLE ONION AND ANCHOVY PIZZA

Pissaladière

From the Provence–Côte d'Azur Region by Philippe Mouchel

❧

*The sunny Côte d'Azur on the coast of France next to Italy is typified
by this pissaladière, a flavoursome French-style pizza much loved as a snack
or as an appetiser served with drinks.*

55 g (2 oz) butter
3 large brown onions,
  very thinly sliced
500 g (1 lb 2 oz) ready-to-use
  bread dough, or a large
  ready-to-use pizza base
3 tablespoons extra-virgin olive oil
20 anchovy fillets, drained of oil

25 black olives, pitted
25 small sprigs thyme,
  about 1 cm (½ in) long
freshly ground black pepper
a little plain (all-purpose) flour
  for dusting

Preheat the oven to 190°C (375°F). Line a baking tray with baking (parchment) paper.

Heat the butter in a large, non-stick frying pan. Add the onions and cook on low heat for about 20 minutes, stirring from time to time. Don't try to cook the onions too quickly or they will burn and taste unpleasant. Allow the onions to cool slightly before using.

If using bread dough, roll out to a thickness of about 5 mm (¼ in). Carefully lift the dough or pizza base onto the prepared tray. Brush with a little oil.

Spread the cooked onions on top of the dough or pizza base, leaving a margin of about 2 cm (¾ in) at the edges. Decorate with the anchovy fillets, making a criss-cross pattern. Arrange the olives and sprigs of thyme in the spaces between the anchovies and season with a little black pepper.

Bake for about 15 minutes or until the pastry is brown and crisp and it smells wonderful. Cut into pieces and serve.

Serves 6–8 as an appetiser with pre-dinner drinks

QUICHE LORRAINE

From the Lorraine Region by Philippe Mouchel

❧

This is perhaps the best-known French dish outside France and can be easily varied by using different cheese, spices and herbs. It's a very traditional dish.

Pastry

125 g (4 oz) butter, cut into pieces

1 egg yolk

a pinch of salt

300 g (10½ oz/2 cups) plain (all-purpose) flour

3 tablespoons water

juice of ½ lemon

Filling

2 egg yolks

2 whole eggs

100 ml (3½ fl oz) milk

300 ml (10 fl oz) pouring cream

salt

finely ground black pepper

2 pinches of freshly grated nutmeg

1 teaspoon butter

100 g (3½ oz) bacon, diced

100 g (3½ oz) grated gruyère cheese (or another cheese of your choice)

To make the pastry, place the butter, egg yolk and salt in a food processor and blend to combine. Add the flour, water and lemon juice and pulse to form a ball. Remove from the food processor, wrap in plastic wrap and refrigerate for at least 30 minutes before using.

Preheat the oven to 230°C (450°F). Grease a 22 cm (8½ in) loose-based flan (tart) tin and line the base with baking (parchment) paper.

Roll out the pastry on a floured surface and use to line the flan tin. Trim the edges and line the pastry with foil. Fill with pastry weights (or use rice or dried beans). Cook for 12 minutes, then carefully remove the foil and weights.

In a bowl, whisk together the yolks, whole eggs, milk and cream. Season to taste with salt, pepper and nutmeg.

Lower the oven temperature to 180°C (350°F).

Melt the butter in a frying pan and cook the bacon for 3 minutes, turning occasionally. Drain the bacon well then scatter over the blind-baked pastry shell. Sprinkle on the cheese then pour in the egg mixture.

Carefully transfer the quiche to the oven and cook for 20–25 minutes, or until the filling is set and the top is golden brown. When cooked, remove from the oven and leave for about 10 minutes before unmoulding.

Serves 6

Calibre 63 à 73 g

OEUFS DE POULES
élevées en plein air
au maïs et au blé

l'œuf ⟶ 0.80 €
le Plateau de 30 Oeufs ⟶ 24.00 €

SILVERBEET GRATIN

Gratin de blettes

From the Alps Region

❧

Many French people eat their main meal of the day at lunchtime, then for dinner they often have a satisfying vegetarian dish such as this lovely silverbeet gratin, an Alpine specialty that uses flavoursome local cheese.

8 silverbeet leaves with
   the stalks, well washed
55 g (2 oz) butter
salt
freshly ground pepper
¼ teaspoon freshly grated nutmeg
125 ml (4½ fl oz/½ cup) cream

20 g (¾ oz) plain (all-purpose)
   flour
300 ml (10 fl oz) milk
a pinch of cayenne pepper
about 65 g (2¼ oz) finely
   grated gruyère cheese
3 tablespoons dried breadcrumbs

Separate the silverbeet stalks and leaves. Cut the stalks into 3 cm (1¼ in) pieces and shred the leaves.

Heat a third of the butter in a saucepan. Add the silverbeet stalks and stir for 3 minutes over medium heat. Season with salt and pepper, cover with water and cook for about 15 minutes, or until soft. Drain well and set aside.

Heat another third of the butter in a different saucepan. Add the shredded silverbeet leaves and cook until wilted. Season with nutmeg, a little salt and pepper and half the cream. Set aside.

Melt the rest of the butter in a saucepan over medium heat. Whisk in the flour and cook for 1 minute. Slowly add the milk, whisking constantly until it forms a smooth white sauce. Season with cayenne pepper, stir in the remaining cream and simmer for 2 minutes. Add the drained silverbeet stalks and mix in about 2 tablespoons of the gruyère cheese.

Spoon the cooked silverbeet leaves into a 25 cm (10 in) gratin dish. Pour on the white sauce, then scatter on the remaining cheese and top with the breadcrumbs. Place under a hot grill (broiler) until lightly browned. Be careful when serving, it's very hot!

Serves 3–4

PROVENÇAL VEGETABLE BAKE

Tian aux légumes Provençals
From the Provence Region

❧

*This excellent Provençal vegetable dish is typical of the region and
a good example of how creative the Mediterraneans are with their vegetables.
'Tian' is actually the name of the cooking dish used. You will need a large
ovenproof dish, made of either porcelain or cast iron.*

125 ml (4½ fl oz/½ cup)
extra-virgin olive oil
1 large brown onion, thinly sliced
1 red or green capsicum (pepper),
seeds removed, thinly sliced
2 medium eggplants (aubergines),
halved and thinly sliced
1 clove garlic, finely chopped
4 medium zucchini (courgettes)

6 tomatoes, cut into 5 mm
(¼ in) slices
salt
freshly ground black pepper
2 tablespoons finely chopped
lemon thyme
2 tablespoons grated parmesan
cheese
3 tablespoons dried breadcrumbs

Heat half the oil in a large, non-stick frying pan. Add the onion and cook,
stirring continuously, for 2 minutes. Add the capsicum and cook for 2 minutes,
stirring again. Add the eggplant and garlic and cook over low heat for about 20
minutes, or until the vegetables are soft.

Preheat the oven to 160°C (315°F).

Peel off the zucchini skin in vertical strips, 1 cm (½ in) apart, so that strips of
skin remain. Cut the zucchini into 5 mm (¼ in) slices.

Transfer the cooked vegetables to an ovenproof dish. Arrange the zucchini and
tomato slices on top of the vegetables in alternate, overlapping rows. Season with
salt and pepper and sprinkle evenly with lemon thyme. Drizzle evenly with the
remaining oil. Bake for about 30 minutes. Sprinkle with parmesan cheese and
breadcrumbs and bake for a further 10 minutes.

Serves 6

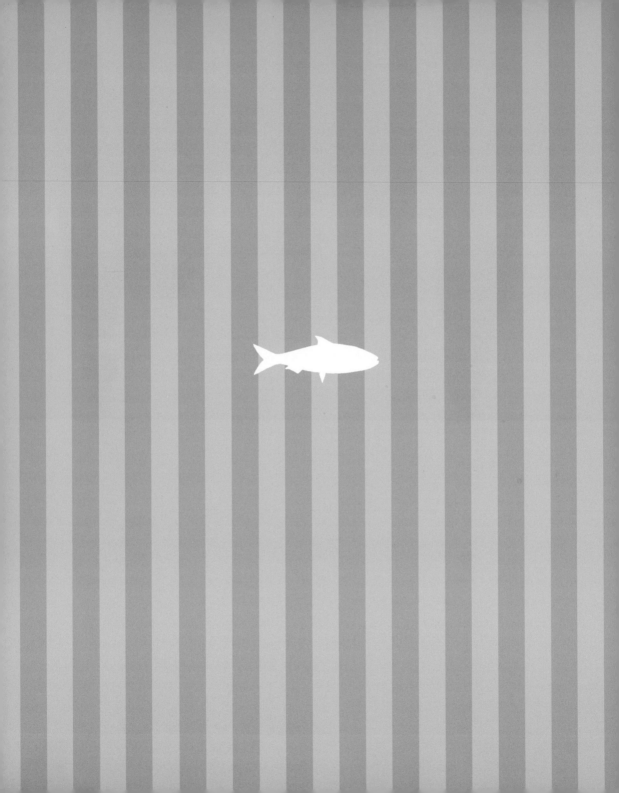

CHAPTER TWO

FISH & SEAFOOD

SCALLOPS THE PARISIAN WAY

Coquilles St Jacques à la Parisienne

From the Paris Region by Philippe Mouchel

❦

The French are very fond of scallops and this delicate dish is a popular family favourite for Sunday lunch. If you have the chance to visit Paris, go to one of the many produce markets and admire the outstanding fish available. This dish looks lovely when presented on empty, clean scallop shells.

12 fresh scallops,
   cleaned and briefly rinsed
8 mushrooms, sliced
250 ml (8½ fl oz/1 cup)
   strong fish stock
20 g (¾ oz) butter
20 g (¾ oz) plain
   (all-purpose) flour
4 tablespoons pouring cream

1 egg yolk
½ lemon
salt
freshly ground pepper
60 g (2 oz) finely grated gruyère
   cheese
2 tablespoons dried breadcrumbs

Place the scallops in a saucepan with the mushrooms. Add the stock and place over medium heat. Bring to a low simmer and cook for 20 seconds. Drain the scallops and mushrooms, and reserve and cool the stock. Divide the scallops and mushrooms among four clean scallop shells and set aside.

Melt the butter in a small saucepan over medium heat. Whisk in the flour and cook for 2 minutes. Slowly add the cool stock, whisking constantly until it thickens. Stir in 2 tablespoons of the cream and cook for a further 2 minutes.

In a small bowl, mix the egg yolk with the rest of the cream. Remove the sauce from the heat and whisk in the cream and egg mixture. Stir in the lemon juice and season with salt and pepper.

Spoon some sauce over the scallops and mushrooms in the shells. Sprinkle with a little grated cheese and breadcrumbs. Place under a hot grill (broiler) until golden brown. (Alternatively, place the shells in a hot oven.) Serve immediately.

Serves 4

RED MULLET WITH TAPENADE AND A FENNEL SALAD

Filets de rouget poêlé à la tapenade, salade de fenouil

From the Provence Region by Philippe Mouchel

❧

Red mullet is a really tasty fish and greatly loved by gourmets. It goes well with strongly flavoured ingredients such as olives, anchovies and fennel. I love it.

80 g (2¾ oz) black olives, pitted
1 teaspoon capers, rinsed
3 anchovy fillets
4 tablespoons olive oil
1 clove garlic, finely chopped
3 basil leaves, finely chopped,
    plus 3 whole leaves
juice of 1 lemon
1 bulb baby fennel, trimmed
    and thinly sliced

¼ medium red (Spanish) onion,
    thinly sliced
4 cherry tomatoes, quartered
2 sprigs fennel leaves, chopped
    (or use dill)
salt
freshly ground black pepper
6 fillets red mullet

To make the tapenade, combine the olives, capers and anchovy fillets in a small food processor and blend to a paste. Continue blending while adding 1½ tablespoons of the oil. Transfer the paste to a bowl and stir in the garlic, chopped basil and a little less than half of the lemon juice. Set aside.

Place the fennel, red onion and cherry tomatoes in a bowl. Roughly tear the whole basil leaves and add them to the bowl with the chopped fennel leaves. Season with a little salt and pepper, half of the remaining oil and the remaining lemon juice. Mix well and set aside.

Heat the remaining oil in a non-stick frying pan over medium–high heat and cook the red mullet fillets, skin side down, for 2 minutes. Turn the fish and cook for 10 seconds.

Divide the salad between two plates. Arrange three fish fillets on each salad and top with a little tapenade. Serve immediately.

Serves 2

FISH QUENELLES

Quenelles de poisson

From the Lyonnais Region by Philippe Mouchel

❦

Philippe Mouchel, a talented chef and my good friend, learned to make fish quenelles when he worked with the world-famous French chef Paul Bocuse in Lyon. This is Philippe's classic and delicious recipe. The quenelles have a unique texture and a wonderful crayfish flavour.

250 ml (8½ fl oz/1 cup) milk
75 g (2½ oz) butter
4 egg yolks
125 g (4 oz/½ cup) plain (all-purpose) flour
250 g (9 oz) delicate white fish fillets
1 egg white
100 g (3½ oz) veal kidney fat, cut into very small pieces (available from good butchers)

a pinch of freshly grated nutmeg
salt
freshly ground pepper
400 ml (13½ fl oz) crayfish bisque (make your own or buy a can)
100 g (3½ oz) crayfish meat, cut into small pieces

Bring the milk and butter to the boil in a medium saucepan. In a bowl, mix the egg yolks with the flour. Add to the milk mixture and whisk until it thickens and forms a mass (called a 'panade'). Transfer the panade to a bowl to cool.

Place the fish and egg white in a food processor and blend to a purée. Add the veal kidney fat and pulse briefly. Add the cool panade gradually, pulsing to incorporate, then season with nutmeg, salt and pepper. Transfer to a bowl and refrigerate for at least 1 hour.

Bring a large, wide saucepan of water to a very gentle simmer. Using two large oval spoons, carefully mould some of the mixture into the traditional oval quenelle shape (practice makes perfect!). You should get 6–8 quenelles from the mixture. Place the quenelles in the hot water to poach for 6–8 minutes, then drain on paper towel.

Preheat the oven to 200°C (400°F). Gently heat the crayfish bisque.

Transfer the quenelles to several small ovenproof dishes – aim for two quenelles per person. Spoon in the crayfish bisque, so it comes three-quarters of the way up the quenelles, and garnish with a little crayfish meat. Bake for 10 minutes, then serve.

Serves 3–4

CRAYFISH STEW

Civet de langouste

From the coast of Languedoc-Roussillon Region by Philippe Mouchel

❦

This special crayfish stew has a real taste of the Mediterranean region, especially when made using Banyuls, a local fortified wine that is very popular as an aperitif.

4 tablespoons extra-virgin olive oil
½ brown onion, chopped
3 tomatoes, peeled, seeded
   and diced
1 clove garlic, chopped
1 bay leaf
4 sprigs parsley
1 x 500 g (1 lb 2 oz) crayfish tail in
   the shell, cut into 6 pieces

salt
freshly ground pepper
20 g (¾ oz) butter
2 teaspoons cognac
80 ml (2½ fl oz/⅓ cup) Banyuls
a pinch of cayenne pepper
4 thin slices prosciutto-style
   ham, roughly torn
a few sprigs chervil

Heat 1 tablespoon of the oil in a non-stick saucepan. Add the onion and cook over medium heat for a few minutes. Add the tomatoes, garlic, bay leaf and parsley, then cover the pan and cook over low heat for 30 minutes.

Season the crayfish pieces with a little salt and pepper.

Heat 2 more tablespoons of oil in a frying pan and cook the crayfish pieces on all sides for a few minutes. Add the butter and when it has melted, baste the crayfish. Add the cognac, bring to the boil, remove the pan away from the stove and flame. Return the pan to the stove, add the Banyuls, bring to the boil and flame once more (again, do this away from the stove). Remove the crayfish pieces from the pan, then boil the liquid until reduced by half.

Add the tomato mixture to the pan and season with cayenne pepper, salt and pepper. Bring to a simmer, return the crayfish pieces to the pan and simmer in the sauce for a few minutes.

Add a few pieces of ham to the sauce and warm gently. Spoon a little sauce onto two plates and divide the crayfish pieces between them. Top each serve with a few pieces of ham, drizzle on the remaining olive oil and garnish with chervil.

Serves 2

RICH BASQUE FISH STEW

Ttoro

From the Basque/Atlantic Region

⚜

Basque cooking is influenced by both French and Spanish cuisine. It is full of colour and strong flavours, such as olive oil, chilli and saffron.

1.5 kg (3 lb 5 oz) firm, whole white fish
4 tablespoons olive oil
1 small leek, thinly sliced
1 small onion, thinly sliced
½ small capsicum (pepper), diced
½ long red chilli, thinly sliced
2 tomatoes, finely diced
1 clove garlic, crushed
1 sprig thyme
2 sprigs parsley
a pinch of saffron threads

150 ml (5 fl oz) dry white wine
salt
freshly ground black pepper
55 g (2 oz) plain (all-purpose) flour
12 scampi
500 g (1 lb 2 oz) mussels, thoroughly scrubbed and beards removed
4 tablespoons chopped parsley
4 slices toasted bread, rubbed with raw garlic

Ask your fishmonger to clean and scale the fish, and to cut it into 5 cm (2 in) pieces. Ask them to remove the fish heads and to cut them into pieces also.

Heat 2 tablespoons of the oil in a large saucepan. Add the leek, onion and fish heads. Cook over medium heat for 5 minutes, stirring occasionally.

Add the capsicum, chilli, tomatoes, garlic, thyme, parsley and saffron and stir well. Add the wine and bring to the boil. Add enough water to cover and season with salt and pepper. Bring to a simmer and cook for 30 minutes, uncovered.

Pat the fish pieces dry and coat lightly with flour.

Heat the remaining oil in a large saucepan and fry the fish pieces for about 1 minute on each side. Add the scampi, then the mussels. Strain the fish stock into the pan, shake well and cover with a lid. Cook over medium heat until the mussels have opened.

Ladle the stew into deep soup plates. Sprinkle with chopped parsley and serve with the garlic toasts.

Serves 6

TROUT WITH PINE NUTS AND CAPERS

Truite Grenobloise

From the Alps Region by Philippe Mouchel

❖

I cooked this beautiful trout dish hundreds of times when I was a young chef working in Paris. It's very easy to do at home.

60 ml (2 fl oz/¼ cup) olive oil

2 slices bread, cut into
   1 cm (½ in) cubes

2 fresh trout, thoroughly
   cleaned inside and out

salt

freshly ground black pepper

3 tablespoons plain
   (all-purpose) flour

85 g (3 oz) butter

3 tablespoons pine nuts

3 tablespoons capers

1 lemon, peeled and cut
   into segments

juice of ½ lemon

3 tablespoons chopped
   parsley

Heat half the oil in a frying pan and fry the bread cubes until golden. Drain on paper towel.

Season the fish with salt and pepper and dust all over with a little flour.

Heat the remaining oil in another frying pan and cook the fish for 4 minutes on each side. Add one-third of the butter to the pan and baste the fish. Transfer the fish to a serving plate and keep warm.

Add the remaining butter to the pan. Stir in the pine nuts and cook for 1 minute until golden brown. Add the capers, lemon segments and lemon juice and reheat. Add the chopped parsley and spoon the sauce over the trout. Scatter the croutons on top and serve.

Serves 2

ROAST SNAPPER WITH MONTPELLIER BUTTER

Daurade rôtie au beurre de Montpellier

From the Languedoc Region

⚜

The sunny city of Montpellier in southern France is a lovely place to visit. There's a great tradition in the region of blending seafood with the produce of the land. Montpellier butter is a very tasty accompaniment and goes well with fish.

one 1 kg (2 lb 3 oz) snapper
  (or other firm white fish),
  scaled and cleaned
sea salt
freshly ground black pepper
3 tablespoons olive oil
2 French shallots, thinly sliced
2 teaspoons fennel seeds
4 sprigs parsley
80 ml (2½ fl oz/⅓ cup)
  dry white wine

Montpellier Butter

55 g (2 oz) butter, softened
1 tablespoon chopped parsley
1 tablespoon chopped chervil
6 tarragon leaves, thinly sliced
1 small gherkin (pickle), finely
  chopped
6 capers, finely chopped
1 anchovy fillet, finely chopped
juice of ¼ lemon
freshly ground black pepper

To make the Montpellier butter, place the butter in a bowl and add the herbs, gherkin, capers, anchovy, lemon juice and a little pepper. Mix with a fork until just combined. Spoon onto a piece of foil, roll up into a neat log and refrigerate until firm.

Preheat the oven to 200°C (400°F).

Make several 1 cm (½ in) deep cuts in the thickest part of both sides of the fish and season with sea salt and pepper.

Pour half the oil in a baking dish large enough to hold the fish. Scatter half the shallots, half the fennel seeds and all the parsley sprigs on the base of the dish. Place the snapper on top and scatter on the remaining shallots and fennel seeds. Drizzle the wine and remaining oil over the fish, cover with foil and bake for 25 minutes.

To serve, discard the parsley stalks and carefully lift the snapper flesh away from the bones. Serve with a slice of Montpellier butter. It's lovely with a tomato salad.

Serves 2

PERCH FILLET WITH ASPARAGUS AND CHABLIS SAUCE

Filet de perche sauce au chablis et aux asperges
From the Burgundy Region

❧

If you are a food and wine lover, Burgundy is one of the top French regions to visit, and Chablis is a most charming village nestled amongst the chardonnay vineyards.

55 g (2 oz) butter	salt
1 French shallot, finely chopped	freshly ground black pepper
2 button mushrooms, thinly sliced	3 tablespoons chablis
2 x 200 g (7 oz) fillets perch	6 fat asparagus tips
(or other lean, flaky-textured fish	2 tablespoons pouring cream
such as rockfish or red snapper)	4 sprigs of chervil

Melt a quarter of the butter in a frying pan over medium heat. Add the shallot and stir for 30 seconds. Add the mushrooms. Top with the fish fillets, season with salt and pepper and pour the chablis around the fish.

Cover the pan with foil or a lid and steam over low heat until just done. It only takes 6–8 minutes.

Meanwhile, steam the asparagus tips until tender.

Transfer the fish and mushrooms to a serving dish or two plates and cover with foil. Bring the cooking liquid to the boil and cook for 2 minutes. Whisk in the remaining butter. When it has all melted, add the asparagus tips to the sauce.

Top the fish with the asparagus and spoon on the sauce. Garnish with chervil sprigs and serve.

Serves 2

PAN-FRIED SALMON WITH BUTTER SAUCE

Saumon poêlé au beurre blanc

From the Loire Valley Region by Philippe Mouchel

⚜

Beurre blanc was the star sauce during my apprenticeship in the Loire Valley and chef Albert Augereau was a master at preparing it. This classic sauce has become less popular because of its butter content, but it's so delicious! The reduction part of the sauce may be made ahead of time, but the cream and butter should not be added until you are ready to serve as the sauce does not reheat well.

2 medium potatoes
10 asparagus spears, trimmed
1 tablespoon vegetable oil
2 salmon cutlets
2 teaspoons butter
salt
freshly ground black pepper

Beurre Blanc Sauce

1 large French shallot or ½ medium
  white onion, finely chopped
60 ml (2 fl oz/¼ cup) dry white
  vinegar
60 ml (2 fl oz/¼ cup) dry white wine
1 teaspoon cracked pepper
1 teaspoon pouring cream
100 g (3½ oz) very cold butter,
  cut into small cubes

To make the beurre blanc sauce, combine the shallot or onion, vinegar, wine and pepper in a small saucepan. Bring to a simmer and cook for 5–10 minutes, or until almost all the liquid has evaporated. Set aside.

Steam the potatoes and asparagus separately, until tender. Meanwhile, heat the oil in a frying pan and cook the salmon for 2 minutes on each side. Add the butter to the pan and when it has melted, baste the salmon. Season with salt and pepper.

While the salmon is cooking, gently reheat the shallot reduction. Add the cream and bring to the boil. Lower the heat to a minimum and whisk in the butter, piece by piece. During this time the sauce must be whisked constantly. It should hold together and be creamy and smooth.

Arrange the salmon on two plates with the asparagus and potatoes. Serve the sauce either on the side of the plate or separately in a sauce boat.

Serves 2

BLUE EYE AND SCALLOPS WITH BUTTER SAUCE

Cabillaud et coquilles St Jacques au beurre blanc
From the Brittany/Loire Valley Regions

❧

The west of France, with the Channel and the Atlantic Ocean, has a wonderful repertoire of excellent fish dishes. I am a native of Western France and when I was young my mother usually preferred to serve a fish dish such as this for special occasions rather than a meat dish.

60 g (2 oz) butter, cut into cubes	2 fillets blue eye (or other firm,
1 French shallot, finely chopped	white fish), skinned
2 tablespoons white wine vinegar	200 g (7 oz) fresh scallops, cleaned
100 ml (3½ fl oz) dry white wine	salt
freshly ground black pepper	1 teaspoon pouring cream
1 zucchini (courgette)	1 sprig dill

Melt 1 teaspoon of the butter in a small saucepan over low heat. Add the shallot and stir for 1 minute. Add the vinegar and 3 tablespoons of the wine, season with black pepper and simmer until the liquid has nearly evaporated. Set aside.

Cut the zucchini into thin slices, and then into thin julienne strips.

Melt another teaspoon of the butter in a medium frying pan over medium heat. Add the zucchini and stir for 20 seconds. Add the fish, cook for 1 minute, then add the scallops. Season with salt and pepper. Add the remaining wine, cover with foil or a lid and cook over low heat for about 2 minutes. Turn the fish over and cook for a further 2 minutes.

Add the cream to the shallot mixture. Place the pan over low heat and slowly whisk in the remaining butter, cube by cube, until melted and smooth.

Place the fish fillets on two warmed plates. Top with a little zucchini, then a few scallops. Spoon on some of the butter sauce, garnish with dill and serve.

Serves 2

POACHED TROUT WITH HOLLANDAISE SAUCE

Truite au bleu hollandaise

From the Alps Region by Philippe Mouchel

❧

The beautiful streams and lakes in the Alps region are teeming with trout, so it has become the specialty of the area. The French often prefer their fish poached rather than pan-fried or deep-fried.

3 litres (101 fl oz/12 cups) cold water
1 medium onion, thinly sliced
1 medium carrot, thinly sliced
a few parsley stalks
1 bay leaf
2 sprigs thyme
10 peppercorns
2 very fresh river trout (not rainbow trout), thoroughly cleaned, inside and out

small handful of parsley leaves
60 ml (2 fl oz/¼ cup) white vinegar

Hollandaise Sauce
85 g (3 oz) butter
1 egg yolk
2 teaspoons hot water
salt
freshly ground black pepper
1 teaspoon lemon juice

Put the water in a large saucepan over medium heat and add the onion and carrot. Use kitchen string to tie the parsley stalks, bay leaf and thyme sprigs together to make a bouquet garni and add to the pan with the peppercorns. Bring to the boil and cook for 10 minutes.

Meanwhile, make the hollandaise sauce. Melt the butter in a small saucepan over low heat until warm, but not hot. Combine the egg yolk and hot water in a bowl set over a saucepan of hot water. Season with a little salt and pepper and whisk for a few minutes until light and fluffy. Remove the bowl from the heat, then very slowly add the warm melted butter, whisking continuously until well incorporated. Stir in the lemon juice.

Carefully place the trout in the hot poaching liquid and heat until close to boiling point. Reduce the heat and poach the fish for 10 minutes. Turn off the heat, add the parsley and leave to stand for 3 minutes.

Heat the vinegar in a small saucepan. Carefully lift the two trout onto a flat dish and spoon on the hot vinegar, which gives them a blueish tinge.

Arrange the trout in deep serving plates with some of the vegetables and 2–3 tablespoons of the cooking liquid. Drizzle on a little hollandaise sauce and serve the remaining sauce in a small bowl on the side.

Serves 2

SAUTÉED CHICKEN WITH TARRAGON CREAM SAUCE AND CARROTS

Poulet sauté à la crème d'estragon et aux carottes

From the Lyon/Central France Regions

⚜

One of the highlights of French cooking is its wonderful variety of poultry dishes. Chicken with tarragon is so French and is often served as a main course at Sunday lunch for the extended family.

1 tablespoon extra-virgin olive oil
8 pieces chicken on the bone
  (thighs or drumsticks)
2 French shallots, finely chopped
60 ml (2 fl oz/¼ cup) dry
  white wine
5 medium carrots, thinly sliced
20 g (¾ oz) butter

60 ml (2 fl oz/¼ cup) water
salt
freshly ground pepper
60 ml (2 fl oz/¼ cup)
  pouring cream
3 tablespoons tarragon
  leaves

Heat the oil in a wide, non-stick saucepan and brown the chicken pieces on all sides. Add the shallots, then stir and cook over low heat for 5 minutes. Add the wine to the pan and bring to a simmer. Cover with foil and a lid and cook over low heat for about 20 minutes.

Meanwhile, put the carrots in a saucepan with the butter and water and season with salt and pepper. Cover the pan and cook for about 10 minutes, or until the carrots are tender.

When ready to serve, add the cream to the chicken and bring to a simmer uncovered, turning the chicken pieces around in the sauce. Stir in 2 tablespoons of the tarragon leaves.

Divide the carrots among four plates and top each with two pieces of chicken. Spoon a little sauce over the top, garnish with the remaining tarragon leaves and serve.

Serves 4

ROAST POUSSIN WITH FRENCH LENTILS

Poussin rôti aux lentilles du Puy

From the Centre of France/Massif Central Region

❧

The delicious and delicate green lentils from the town of Le Puy-en-Velay are world famous and loved by all, from the most humble cook to the top French chefs.

2 poussins (baby chickens)
2 tablespoons olive oil
2 sprigs thyme, finely chopped
freshly ground black pepper

French Lentils

2 teaspoons butter
30 g (1 oz) bacon, finely chopped
¼ onion, finely chopped
2 sprigs thyme
a few sprigs parsley

½ bay leaf
½ carrot, diced
3 tablespoons diced celery
140 g (5 oz/¾ cup) puy lentils
1 clove garlic
375 ml (12½ fl oz/1½ cups)
  chicken stock
salt
freshly ground black pepper
3 tablespoons chopped parsley

To prepare the lentils, heat the butter in a saucepan. Add the bacon and fry for 1 minute. Add the onion, stir well and fry for 1 minute.

Use kitchen string to tie the thyme, parsley and bay leaf together.

Add the carrot and celery to the pan and stir well. Add the herbs, lentils and whole garlic clove. Add the stock and bring to a simmer. Cover with a lid and cook over low heat for about 40 minutes, or until the lentils are tender.

The lentils may be prepared ahead of time and gently reheated. Season with salt and pepper and stir in the chopped parsley just before serving.

Rub the poussins all over with the oil and the chopped thyme. Season with pepper, cover and refrigerate until 10 minutes before cooking.

Preheat the oven to 160°C (315°F).

Place the poussins in a small roasting tin and roast for about 35 minutes, turning the birds a couple of times during the cooking. Rest for 10 minutes before carving and serve with the lentils.

Serves 2–4

BRESSE CHICKEN WITH MOREL MUSHROOMS

Poulet de Bresse aux morilles

From the Franche-Comté Region (east of Lyon)

❧

The chickens from around the town of Bourg-en-Bresse are considered by many to be the finest in France for flavour and texture. Select the best-quality chicken you can find for this dish. Dried morels are readily available from good supermarkets and delicatessens. They need to be rinsed and soaked before using. Fresh morels are usually fairly clean, but brush away any visible dirt.

10 g (⅓ oz) dried morels or
   100 g (3½ oz) fresh morels
10 baby carrots
20 g (¾ oz) butter
2 corn-fed chicken breast fillets
salt
freshly ground black pepper

1 French shallot, finely
   chopped
3 tablespoons strong veal stock
2 tablespoons pouring cream
2 tablespoons chopped parsley
juice of ¼ lemon

Preheat the oven to 130°C (250°F).

If using dried morels, put them in a bowl and cover with lukewarm water. Stir to wash the grit off. Carefully lift the morels from the water and transfer them to a clean bowl. Cover with cold water and leave to soak for 15 minutes.

Put the carrots in a saucepan with a little water and cook until just tender.

Heat the butter in a non-stick frying pan and brown the chicken fillets for 2 minutes on each side. Season with salt and pepper. Transfer to a small ovenproof dish and bake for 15 minutes.

Add the shallot to the frying pan and stir for 1 minute. Drain the morels, reserving the liquid. Add to the pan, season with salt and pepper and sweat for 5 minutes over medium heat. Add the soaking liquid and bring to a simmer. Add the stock and cream and simmer until the liquid has reduced by half.

Add the chicken and carrots to the morel sauce. Baste the chicken with the sauce for 30 seconds. Add the chopped parsley and lemon juice, stir and serve.

Serves 2

CHICKEN FRICASSÉE WITH ARTICHOKES

Poulet aux artichauts

From the Provence Region

❧

The sun shines abundantly at the border of the northern part of Provence, and the local artichokes and tomatoes make a superb, delicate accompaniment to the region's many fine chicken dishes.

3 small globe artichokes
1 slice lemon
1 tablespoon extra-virgin olive oil
2 chicken drumsticks on the bone, skin on
2 chicken thighs on the bone, skin on
salt
freshly ground black pepper

1 teaspoon coriander seeds
½ teaspoon fennel seeds
½ small brown onion, finely chopped
1 teaspoon tomato paste (concentrated purée)
3 tablespoons dry white wine
2 tomatoes, finely diced
2 tablespoons chopped parsley

Cut two-thirds off the top of the artichokes, using a serrated knife. Then use a paring knife to carefully trim away all the leaves so you are left with the artichoke heart. Trim the artichoke stalks, leaving about 2 cm (¾ in). Using a melon baller or spoon, remove the hairy part of the heart, then cut the heart into quarters. Rub the clean artichoke pieces with a slice of lemon to prevent discolouring, then place them in a bowl of cold water until required.

Heat the oil in a medium frying pan and brown the chicken pieces for 2 minutes on each side. Season the chicken with salt and pepper.

Drain the artichoke pieces, add them to the pan and stir for 2 minutes. Add the coriander and fennel seeds and stir briefly, then add the onion and cook for 3 minutes. Stir in the tomato paste and white wine and bring to the boil. Stir in the tomatoes and bring to a simmer. Cover with a lid and cook over low heat for 15–20 minutes.

To serve, spoon a little sauce and some artichoke pieces onto two plates. Top with the chicken pieces, sprinkle with parsley and serve.

Serves 2

CHICKEN AND PRAWN CASSEROLE

Poulet aux gambas

From the Languedoc/Roussillon Region

❧

It's very Mediterranean to cook chicken and prawns (shrimp) together, especially with spices such as chilli and saffron (as in a paella). Gambas are large prawns – they are fleshy and succulent.

4 tablespoons extra-virgin olive oil

1 brown onion, chopped

4 chicken pieces on the bone (thighs are good)

salt

freshly ground pepper

1 mild green chilli, thinly sliced

2 large tomatoes, peeled, seeded and chopped

3 tablespoons vermouth

a pinch of saffron threads

8 raw king prawns (jumbo shrimp), shells on

4 tablespoons pine nuts, roasted and finely chopped

3 tablespoons chopped parsley

2 cloves garlic, chopped

Heat 1 tablespoon of the oil in a frying pan and cook the onion over low heat for 5 minutes.

Season the chicken pieces with salt and pepper. Heat another 2 tablespoons of oil in a wide saucepan and brown the chicken pieces all over. Add the onion to the pan, together with the chilli, tomato, vermouth and saffron. Bring to a simmer, cover with a lid and cook for 20 minutes. Turn the chicken pieces over once during the cooking.

Heat the remaining oil in a large frying pan and cook the prawns for 1 minute on each side. Add the prawns to the pan with the chicken, stir gently and cook for 2 minutes more. Stir in the pine nuts, parsley and garlic and serve immediately.

Serves 4

POACHED CHICKEN WITH VEGETABLES

Poule au pot

From the Béarn/Pyrénées Region by Elizabeth Kerdelhué

❧

The French, me included, adore their poule au pot. In the depths of winter it is really lovely comfort food. Poule au pot is easy to prepare and very healthy. The tasty cooking broth is served separately as a soup, to which small pasta is sometimes added.

1.8 kg (4 lb) free-range chicken,
   skin on or off, according to taste
a few sprigs thyme
a few sprigs parsley
1 bay leaf
1 medium brown onion
3 cloves
8 black peppercorns
salt
freshly ground black pepper
4 medium carrots

4 medium turnips
2 leeks, cut into
   10 cm (4 in) lengths
2 stalks celery, cut into
   10 cm (4 in) lengths
2 teaspoons mustard
2 tablespoons red wine vinegar
125 ml (4 fl oz/½ cup) olive oil
6 gherkins (pickles), thinly sliced
2 tablespoons chopped parsley

Put the chicken in a large pot, cover with water and place it on medium heat.

Use kitchen string to tie the thyme, parsley and bay leaf together to make a bouquet garni. Stud the onion with the cloves and add to the pot with the bouquet garni and peppercorns. Season with salt and pepper.

Add the vegetables to the pot, bring to a simmer and cook for about 50 minutes. Remove surface foam from time to time with a large spoon or skimmer.

In a small bowl, mix the mustard with a little salt and pepper. Whisk in the vinegar, then add the oil, whisking continuously. Stir in the gherkins and parsley.

Transfer the chicken and vegetables to a platter and serve with the dressing either poured over the top or in a separate bowl. Serve the broth separately, with or without pasta.

Serves 4

CHICKEN BURGUNDY

Coq au vin

From the Burgundy Region

❦

This is one of the first classic French dishes I learned to prepare as an eighteen-year-old chef in Paris. There are several versions of the dish and if you have time you can marinate the chicken in the wine overnight.

20 small onions (pickling onions)
55 g (2 oz) butter
100 g (3½ oz) bacon, thinly sliced
250 g (9 oz) mushrooms
8 chicken pieces on the bone
   (e.g. 4 drumsticks and 4 thighs)
sea salt
freshly ground black pepper
2 tablespoons cognac
1 heaped tablespoon plain
   (all-purpose) flour

400 ml (13½ fl oz) good-
   quality red wine
1 sprig thyme
a few sprigs parsley
1 bay leaf
1 clove garlic
2 tablespoons tomato paste
   (concentrated purée)
2 tablespoons chopped parsley

Put the onions in a saucepan with plenty of cold water, bring to the boil, cook for 2 minutes then drain well.

Melt half the butter in a large ovenproof saucepan or casserole dish. Add the onions and brown them over medium heat for a few minutes. Add the bacon and stir well for 2 minutes. Add the mushrooms and cook for 4–5 minutes until the mushrooms are soft. Transfer the onions, bacon and mushrooms to a dish.

Add the remaining butter to the pan and brown the chicken pieces over high heat for a few minutes. Season with salt and pepper and stir well. Drain off excess fat into a bowl and discard.

Add the cognac to the pan, remove the pan away from the stove and carefully flame the chicken pieces. Stir well, then sprinkle on the flour. Pour in the red wine and shake the pan.

Use kitchen string to tie the thyme, parsley and bay leaf together to make a bouquet garni. Add to the pan, together with the garlic and tomato paste, return the pan to the heat and stir well. Bring to a slow simmer, cover with a lid and cook for about 20 minutes.

Turn the chicken pieces over, add the mushrooms, bacon and onions to the pan and simmer for a further 10 minutes. Check the seasoning, sprinkle with chopped parsley and serve.

Serves 4

Note: If you prefer a thicker sauce, pour it into a separate saucepan and boil until reduced to your liking.

CHICKEN CASSEROLE COOKED IN RIESLING

Poulet au riesling

From the Alsace Region

❧

The white wines of Alsace made with riesling grapes are outstanding, and in true French tradition, a region with great wine also offers wonderful gastronomy. This dish is a fine example of a festive Alsatian dish.

12 parsley stalks
1 bay leaf
2 sprigs thyme
4 chicken drumsticks
   (skin on or off)
4 chicken thighs
   (skin on or off)
salt
freshly ground black pepper
1 tablespoon olive oil

20 g (¾ oz) butter
2 French shallots, chopped
2 tablespoons cognac or brandy
200 ml (7 fl oz) Alsace riesling
a little grated nutmeg (optional)
300 g (10½ oz) baby mushrooms
juice of ½ lemon
100 ml (3½ fl oz) pouring cream
2 egg yolks
3 tablespoons chopped parsley

Use kitchen string to tie the parsley stalks, bay leaf and thyme together. Season the chicken pieces with salt and pepper. Heat the oil and half the butter in a large heavy-based saucepan. Brown the chicken pieces over high heat for 2–3 minutes. Add the shallots, shake the pan and cook for 2 minutes.

Add the cognac to the pan, stir well, remove the pan away from the stove, then carefully flame the chicken pieces. When the flame dies down, add the wine, nutmeg and herbs. Return the pan to the stove, bring to a slow simmer, cover with a lid and cook for about 25 minutes.

Meanwhile, melt the remaining butter in a frying pan. Sauté the mushrooms until just tender. Add them to the chicken and simmer for 3 minutes. Stir in the lemon juice.

In a medium bowl, whisk together the cream and egg yolks. Pour in 250 ml (8½ fl oz/1 cup) of the hot cooking liquid from the chicken, whisking continuously. Pour the mixture back into the pan and stir gently over low heat for a few minutes (it must not boil). Discard the bouquet garni, add the chopped parsley and serve.

Serves 4

GRILLED DUCK WITH SAUTÉED POTATOES AND CURLY SALAD

Canard grillé, pommes de terre sautées, salade frisée

From the Languedoc Region by Philippe Mouchel

⚜

This duck recipe is very simple to prepare and a lovely example of a rustic French dish that can be served when a couple of friends come to dinner.

3 duck legs

1 tablespoon sea salt

freshly ground black pepper

3 teaspoons finely grated lemon zest

2 tablespoons goose fat (available from specialist butchers and good delicatessens)

2 large potatoes, peeled and cut into 1 cm (½ in) cubes

2 cloves garlic, 1 crushed and 1 finely chopped

1 red (Spanish) onion, cut into long thin pieces

salt

freshly ground black pepper

100 g (3½ oz) mushrooms, quartered

1 tablespoon chopped thyme

1 tablespoon rosemary leaves

20 g (¾ oz) butter

1 teaspoon dijon mustard

1 tablespoon cherry vinegar or other vinegar

3 tablespoons olive oil

3 cups curly endive (frisée), roughly torn

3 sprigs thyme, to garnish

Preheat the grill (broiler) to high.

Rub the duck legs all over with sea salt, paying special attention to the skin side. Place the duck legs on a rack set in a roasting tin. Season the duck skin with pepper and lemon zest. Place under the hot grill and cook until the skins have browned a little. Turn off the grill element and set the oven temperature to 200°C (440°F). Cook the duck legs for about 30 minutes.

Meanwhile, heat the goose fat in a large frying pan. Add the potato and stir over medium heat for 2–3 minutes. Add the crushed garlic and the onion and stir for 2 minutes. Season with salt and pepper. Add the mushrooms and cook for about 8 minutes, or until the potatoes and mushrooms are tender. Add the thyme, rosemary and butter.

In a large salad bowl mix the chopped garlic clove with the mustard, cherry vinegar and a little salt and pepper. Whisk in the oil. Add the curly endive to the bowl and toss well in the dressing.

Divide the potatoes among three plates. Top with a duck leg, garnish with a sprig of thyme and serve with the endive salad.

Serves 3

une baguette

(a) pas trop cuite
(b) plutôt bien cuite
(c) coupée en deux

ROAST DUCK FILLET WITH CHERRIES

Canard aux cerises

From the Pyrénées Region

❧

The scenery in the Pyrénées mountain ranges is stunning. Fruit groves thrive in the valleys between the peaks, and during the hot summers the local sweet cherries make a superb accompaniment to duck, one of the most popular festive dishes of the region.

2–3 medium potatoes,
   peeled and quartered
80 ml (2½ fl oz/⅓ cup) milk
20 g (¾ oz) butter
2 duck breast fillets, skin on
salt
freshly ground black pepper
1 tablespoon olive oil
2 tablespoons port or red wine

2 tablespoons fresh orange juice
2 tablespoons veal glaze
   (available from good butchers
   and delicatessens)
12–20 cherries, pitted just
   before using
2 tablespoons chopped parsley

Preheat the oven to 150°C (300°F).

Boil the potatoes in lightly salted water until tender, then drain well.

Bring the milk and butter to the boil in a medium saucepan. Push the drained potatoes through a mouli or sieve into the hot milk. Stir well. Set the potato purée aside and keep warm.

Meanwhile, use a sharp knife to score the skin of the duck fillets in a criss-cross pattern. Season with salt and pepper.

Heat the oil in small roasting tin and brown the duck fillets, skin side down, for about 3 minutes. Turn the fillets over, then transfer to the oven for about 10 minutes.

When the duck fillets are cooked, transfer them to a warm plate and cover with foil.

Discard the excess fat from the pan, then add the port and bring to the boil.

Add the orange juice and bring to a simmer. Add the veal glaze, return to a simmer, then add the pitted cherries and heat them through.

Just before serving, gently reheat the potato. Divide the potato between two deep plates and arrange a duck fillet on top. Garnish with cherries, spoon on the sauce, sprinkle with chopped parsley and serve.

Serves 2

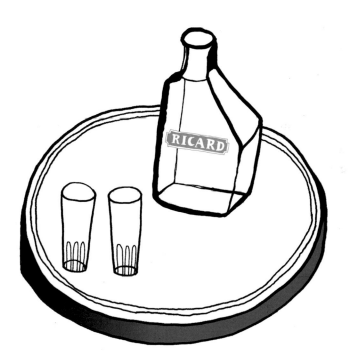

DUCK CASSEROLE IN RED WINE

Daube de canard

From the Gascogne/Pyrénées Region by Philippe Mouchel

❧

A casserole of duck legs cooked slowly in red wine and flavoured with aromatic herbs, orange zest and vegetables is called a 'daube'. It is one of my favourite dishes to enjoy with a good red wine on a cold winter's evening.

3 duck legs
250 ml (8½ fl oz/1 cup) good-
quality red wine
1 medium onion, diced
1 medium carrot, diced
2 cloves garlic, crushed
2 sprigs thyme
1 bay leaf

a few pieces orange zest
salt
freshly ground pepper
a little olive oil
500 g (1 lb 2 oz) baby carrots
2 tablespoons chopped parsley

Put the duck legs in a bowl with the wine, onion, carrot, garlic, thyme, bay leaf and orange zest. Cover with plastic wrap and marinate overnight in the refrigerator.

Preheat the oven to 160°C (315°F).

Remove the duck legs from the marinade and pat them dry with paper towel. Season with salt and pepper. Heat a little oil in a cast-iron saucepan or casserole dish and brown the duck legs on all sides. Use a slotted spoon to remove the vegetables and herbs from the marinade. Add them to the pan and stir for a few minutes. Pour in the marinade, stir and bring to a low simmer. Cover the pan with a lid and bake in the oven for about 1½ hours.

Meanwhile, steam the baby carrots for a couple of minutes.

When the duck legs are almost cooked, remove them from the pan and strain the sauce, discarding the herbs and vegetables. Return the duck legs to the pan and pour in the sauce. Add the carrots, cover the pan and return to the oven for 15 minutes.

Serve each duck leg topped with carrots. Spoon the sauce over the top and serve sprinkled with chopped parsley.

Serves 3

CASSOULET

From the Gascogne Region by Philippe Mouchel

⚜

Cassoulet is a hearty dish of confit duck, baked beans and various pork cuts. It is one of the most popular French winter classics and features on restaurant menus in most family restaurants between Montpellier and Bordeaux. Confit duck and duck fat are available from butchers and good delicatessens.

1 tablespoon duck fat
(or butter or olive oil)
40 g (1½ oz) diced celery
40 g (1½ oz) diced carrot
40 g (1½ oz) diced onion
1 clove garlic
1 cup coco or haricot beans,
soaked overnight in cold water
3 tablespoons dry white wine
1 teaspoon tomato paste
(concentrated purée)
1 bay leaf

2 sprigs thyme
salt
freshly ground black pepper
1 tablespoon olive oil
1–2 Toulouse sausages, or good-
quality pork sausages
200 g (7 oz) cooked pork knuckle
200 g (7 oz) cooked pork belly
2 confit duck legs
50 g (1¾ oz/½ cup) dried
breadcrumbs
3 tablespoons chopped parsley

Preheat the oven to 150°C (300°F).

Heat the duck fat in an ovenproof dish over medium heat. Add the vegetables and garlic clove and sauté for a few minutes. Drain the soaked beans and add them to the dish. Add the wine, stir well and bring to the boil. Add enough water to cover and bring to a simmer. Add the tomato paste, bay leaf and thyme and season with a little salt and pepper. Cover with a lid and cook for 1–1½ hours, or until the beans are almost cooked.

Heat the oil in a frying pan and brown the sausages all over. Add them to the ovenproof dish, along with the pork knuckle, pork belly and duck legs. Shake the dish to distribute the beans evenly, then sprinkle on the breadcrumbs.

Return the dish to the oven and cook, uncovered, for 30 minutes until the breadcrumbs are crisp and brown.

Sprinkle with chopped parsley and serve. French people love to eat cassoulet with mustard but my wife doesn't!

Serves 2–3

CHARCUTERIE FINE

RABBIT STEW WITH PRUNES

Lapin aux pruneaux

From the Béarn/Pyrénées Region by Philippe Mouchel

❧

*Rabbit was an extremely popular meat during my youth in rural France.
My family kept rabbits in the backyard, and we fed them with vegetable scraps
and used the manure to fertilise our vegetable garden.*

18 pitted prunes
375 ml (12½ fl oz/1½ cups)
  good-quality red wine
1 tablespoon honey
1 cinnamon stick
1 star anise
1 x 1.5 kg (3 lb 5 oz) rabbit,
  cut into 6–8 pieces
salt
freshly ground black pepper

1 tablespoon olive oil
20 g (¾ oz) butter
1 small brown onion, diced
1 small carrot, diced
3 sprigs thyme
1 slice pain d'épice
  (spiced honey bread)
3 tablespoons chopped parsley

Preheat the oven to 150°C (300°F).

Put the prunes in a bowl. Combine the wine, honey, cinnamon stick and star
anise in a saucepan. Bring to the boil then pour over the prunes.

Season the rabbit pieces with salt and pepper. Heat the oil and half the butter
in an ovenproof saucepan or casserole dish and brown the rabbit pieces all over.
Tip any excess fat out of the pan and add the remaining butter. Stir in the onion
and carrot, cover with a lid and cook for a few minutes.

Add the soaked prunes, together with their soaking liquid and spices. Finally,
add the thyme and pain d'épice, which will soften and thicken the sauce as it
cooks. Cover the pan and cook for about 2 hours, stirring a couple of times
during cooking. When cooked, the rabbit meat should fall away from the bones.

Sprinkle with chopped parsley and serve.

Serves 6

RABBIT CASSEROLE WITH CAPSICUM AND OLIVES

Lapin aux poivrons et aux olives

From the Northwest Provence Region by Philippe Mouchel

✤

Wild Provençal herbs and wild rabbits are both plentiful around the incredible Mont Ventoux, one of the highest mountains in the north of Provence.

1 red capsicum (pepper)
6 very small pickling onions, peeled
6 rabbit pieces, on the bone
salt
freshly ground black pepper
4 tablespoons extra-virgin olive oil

4 cloves garlic
2 slices bacon, cut into batons
20 black olives
1 small red chilli, roughly chopped
1 sprig rosemary, roughly chopped
100 ml (3½ fl oz) dry white wine
250 ml (8½ fl oz/1 cup) strong chicken or rabbit stock

Preheat the oven to 200°C (400°F). Wrap the capsicum in foil and bake in the oven for about 20 minutes. Remove from the oven, carefully open the foil and, when cool enough to handle, peel the capsicum. Cut it in half, remove the seeds and cut each half into three pieces.

Reduce the oven temperature to 160°C (315°F).

Put the onions in a saucepan with plenty of cold water and bring to the boil. Boil for 2 minutes then drain well.

Season the rabbit with salt and pepper. Heat 2 tablespoons of the oil in a cast-iron casserole dish and brown the rabbit. Add the capsicum, onions, garlic, bacon, olives, chilli and rosemary. Stir well, cover and cook over low heat for 10 minutes.

Add the wine to the pan, bring to the boil and cook until the liquid is reduced to about 2 tablespoons. Add the stock, bring to a simmer, cover with a lid and bake in the oven for about 1½ hours, or until the rabbit is cooked.

Lift the rabbit pieces onto a serving plate. Add the remaining 2 tablespoons of olive oil to the pot with the sauce and vegetables. Bring to the boil and cook for a few minutes to thicken it.

Spoon the vegetables and sauce over the rabbit and serve.

Serves 2

RABBIT WITH A DIJON MUSTARD SAUCE

Lapin à la moutarde de Dijon
From the Burgundy Region

❧

Dijon, the capital of Burgundy, is a great city to visit, not only for its splendid architecture, but because of its world-famous mustard.

6 rabbit hind legs
a little sea salt
freshly ground black pepper
a little plain (all-purpose)
    flour for dusting
2 tablespoons olive oil
20 g (¾ oz) butter
a few sprigs thyme, chopped
150 g (5½ oz) bacon, finely
    chopped
1 bay leaf
2 cloves garlic, crushed

1 medium brown onion,
    chopped
150 ml (5 fl oz) dry white wine
200 g (7 oz) mushrooms,
    halved or quartered,
    depending on size
2 tablespoons Dijon mustard
2 tablespoons pouring cream
1 egg yolk
2 tablespoons chopped parsley

Preheat the oven to 150°C (300°C).

Season the rabbit legs with a little salt and pepper and dust with a little flour.

Heat the oil and butter in an ovenproof casserole dish over medium heat and brown the rabbit legs all over. Add the thyme, bacon, bay leaf, garlic and onion and stir well for 3–5 minutes. Stir in the wine, then add the mushrooms and stir again. Cover with a lid and cook for 1–1½ hours.

Transfer the casserole dish to the stove top over low heat. In a bowl, whisk together the mustard, cream and egg yolk. Slowly stir this mixture into the hot casserole, taking care not to let the sauce boil. Cook over low heat for 5 minutes for the mustard flavour to infuse the rabbit.

Divide the rabbit pieces among six plates, spoon on the sauce and sprinkle with chopped parsley. Serve with your choice of vegetables.

Serves 6

WILD RABBIT WITH MUSHROOMS

Lapin de Garenne aux champignons

From the South of the Loire/Centre Region by Philippe Mouchel

❦

Wild rabbit abounds in the forested rural regions south of the Loire. In autumn and winter, rabbits feature on the table of many farmhouses and the favourite accompaniment is wild mushrooms. I prepare this dish using field mushrooms mixed with a few Swiss browns and shiitake mushrooms.

1 wild rabbit (about 1 kg/2 lb 3 oz), cut into 8 pieces
salt
freshly ground pepper
2 tablespoons olive oil
55 g (2 oz) butter
3 cloves garlic, peeled and crushed
3 French shallots, diced
1 stalk celery, diced

400 g (14 oz) mixed mushrooms, quartered
150 ml (5 fl oz) dry white wine
250 ml (8½ fl oz/1 cup) strong veal or rabbit stock
1 sprig thyme
10 green peppercorns
1 tablespoon tarragon leaves

Preheat the oven to 150°C (300°F).

Season the rabbit with salt and pepper. Heat the oil in a cast-iron saucepan or casserole dish and brown the rabbit on all sides. Add about a third of the butter to the pan, then the garlic, shallots, celery and about 10 of the quartered mushrooms. Stir well, cover and cook over low heat for about 5 minutes.

Add the wine to the pan, bring to the boil and boil for 2 minutes. Add the stock, thyme and peppercorns, cover with a lid and bake for about 2 hours, or until the rabbit is tender, stirring once or twice during the cooking.

Fifteen minutes before you are ready to serve, heat another third of the butter in a frying pan. Add the remaining mushrooms and sauté until just tender. Set aside and keep warm.

Transfer the rabbit pieces to a dish, and cover with foil to keep warm.

Reduce the sauce by half, then stir in the remaining butter. Spoon the sauce and mushrooms over the rabbit pieces, garnish with tarragon leaves and serve.

Serves 3

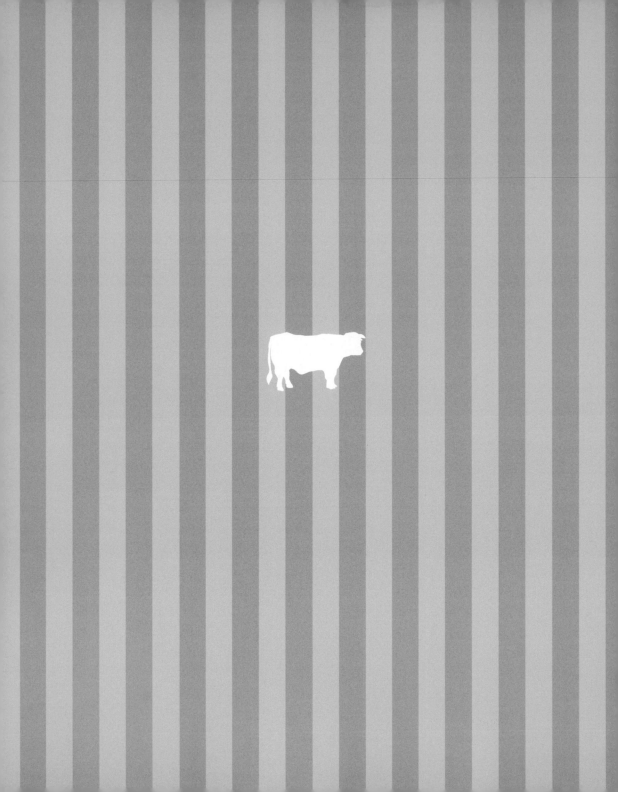

CHAPTER FOUR

⚜

BEEF, LAMB & PORK

EYE FILLET STEAK WITH BÉARNAISE SAUCE

Tournedos sauce béarnaise

From the Pyrénées/Béarn Region by Philippe Mouchel

❧

The delicious béarnaise sauce that is served with this steak was named after the region of Béarn in the north-west of the Pyrénées. If you prefer, cook the steaks on a barbecue (outdoor grill).

4 x 150 g (5½ oz) eye fillet steaks
   (or another steak of your choice)
salt
freshly ground black pepper
1 tablespoon olive oil
1 teaspoon butter

Béarnaise Sauce
2 French shallots, finely chopped
2 tablespoons white wine vinegar

2 tablespoons tarragon leaves
2 tablespoons white wine
4 black peppercorns, crushed
125 g (4 oz) butter, cut into
   small cubes
2 egg yolks
salt
freshly ground black pepper

To make the béarnaise sauce, combine the shallots, vinegar, half the tarragon, the white wine and peppercorns in a saucepan. Bring to a simmer and cook until the liquid has reduced to about 1 tablespoon.

Meanwhile, melt the butter in a small saucepan over low heat.

Place the egg yolks in a medium metal or glass bowl and whisk in the shallot reduction. Sit the bowl over a saucepan of hot water, taking care that the bowl doesn't touch the water. Keep the pan over low heat, as the water must be hot but not boiling. Continue whisking the yolks briskly until they become thick and foamy. After about 5 minutes they should have doubled in volume.

Remove from the saucepan and very slowly pour in the melted butter, whisking continuously until well incorporated. The finished sauce should be creamy but not too runny. Add the rest of the tarragon and season with salt and pepper.

Season the steaks with salt and pepper. Heat the oil in a frying pan and cook the steaks over high heat for 3–5 minutes on each side, or to your liking. Towards the end of the cooking, add the butter to the pan and baste the steaks. Season with salt and pepper and serve on hot plates. Serve the sauce separately.

Serves 4

ROAST BEEF FILLET WITH FRENCH-STYLE PEAS

Rôti de boeuf et petits pois à la Française

From the Limousin Region by Philippe Mouchel

✦

The Limousin region in the heart of France is famous for its superb cattle breed of the same name. The garnish of peas cooked with lettuce is a classic and much loved by the French.

1 x 600 g (1 lb 5 oz) beef eye fillet, tied with kitchen string
salt
cracked black pepper
1 tablespoon olive oil
45 g (1½ oz) butter
1 French shallot, chopped
100 ml (3½ fl oz) red wine
2 tablespoons veal glaze (available from good butchers and delicatessens)
3 tablespoons water
1 sprig thyme

French-style Peas
1 tablespoon olive oil
55 g (2 oz) butter
1 medium brown onion, sliced
1 cos (romaine) lettuce heart, washed and cut into bite-sized pieces, plus a few extra small cos lettuce leaves for garnish (optional)
3 slices prosciutto, cut into pieces
1 clove garlic, finely chopped
500 g (1 lb 2 oz) peas
1 sprigs thyme
250 ml (8½ fl oz/1 cup) chicken stock

Preheat the oven to 180°C (350°F).

Season the beef with salt and pepper. Heat the oil and 1 tablespoon of the butter in a roasting tin, then brown the meat on all sides, basting well. Transfer to the oven for 15–20 minutes, or until cooked to your liking. Remove the string, wrap the meat in foil and leave to rest for 10 minutes.

Tip the cooking fat out of the roasting tin then add another tablespoon of butter. Add the shallot and stir over medium heat for 2 minutes. Add the red wine and boil until reduced to about 2 tablespoons. Add the veal glaze and water and bring to the boil. Season with a little cracked pepper and add the thyme. Tip the sauce into a smaller saucepan and keep hot.

To prepare the French-style peas, heat the oil and 2 tablespoons of the butter in a saucepan. Add the onion and cook for 5 minutes. Add the lettuce, prosciutto, garlic, peas, thyme and chicken stock and simmer for 10 minutes.

When ready to serve, reheat the beef in a frying pan with the remaining butter for 1–2 minutes. Carve into 8 slices. Divide the peas among four plates and top with slices of beef. If you wish, add a little extra butter to the hot sauce, then spoon it over the beef. Garnish with lettuce leaves, if using, and serve at once.

Serves 4

BEEF FILLET WITH TRUFFLES AND FOIE GRAS

Filet de boeuf aux truffes et foie gras

From the Périgord Region

❧

*Every year French gourmets look forward to the truffle season, which starts
with the first frost and finishes with the last (that is, from November to February).
If you are able to source a fresh truffle, then do try this classic dish.*

2 medium potatoes,
   peeled and quartered
60 ml (2 fl oz/¼ cup) milk
55 g (2 oz) butter
2 x 200 g (7 oz) eye fillet steaks
2 teaspoons cracked
   black pepper
salt

2 teaspoons olive oil
1 small French shallot, finely
   chopped
2 tablespoons madeira
60 ml (2 fl oz/¼ cup) strong
   veal stock
10 g (⅓ oz) black truffle, thinly sliced
2 x 20 g (¾ oz) slices foie gras

Boil the potatoes in lightly salted water until tender, then drain well.

Bring the milk to the boil in a medium saucepan. Push the drained potatoes
through a mouli or sieve onto the hot milk. Stir well, then mix in 2 tablespoons
of the butter. Set the potato purée aside and keep warm.

Season the steaks with cracked pepper and salt. Heat the oil and 1 teaspoon
of the remaining butter in a small frying pan. Fry the steaks over high heat for
3–5 minutes on each side, or to your liking. Transfer the steaks to a warm plate
and cover with foil.

Add another teaspoon of butter to the pan. Add the shallot and stir for 2 minutes
over medium heat. Add the madeira and bring to the boil. Add the stock, return
to the boil and boil for 1 minute. Add the rest of the butter and season to taste.
Stir in the sliced truffles.

Just before serving, gently reheat the potato. Divide the potato between two
plates and place a steak on top. Arrange a slice of foie gras on top of each steak,
spoon on a little sauce and serve.

Serves 2

BEEF RIB EYE WITH RED WINE SAUCE AND VEGETABLE PURÉE

Côte de boeuf sauce au vin rouge purée de légumes
From the Limousin/Centre Region

❧

If you're looking for a great dish to serve with a special bottle of red wine, this is it.
It's easy to prepare, but take care not to overcook the beef, and make sure you
rest it for at least 5 minutes before carving.

2 teaspoons olive oil
1 beef rib eye, 400–500 g
  (about 1 lb)
250 g (9 oz) peas
2 small carrots,
  cut into small pieces
30 g (1 oz) butter

salt
freshly ground pepper
1 French shallot, finely
  chopped
2 tablespoons red wine
60 ml (2 fl oz/¼ cup) strong
  beef stock

Preheat the oven to 200°C (400°F).

Heat the oil in a roasting tin and brown each side of the rib eye for about
2 minutes. Transfer to the oven and cook for 10–15 minutes, or to your liking.

Cook the peas and carrots in boiling water in separate saucepans. Drain each
well, then blend each separately with a little of the butter to form a purée.
Season with salt and pepper and keep them warm in the saucepans.

When the rib eye is cooked, transfer it to a warm plate, cover with foil and leave
to rest for about 5 minutes.

Melt the remaining butter in the roasting tin. Add the shallot and cook over low
heat for 2 minutes. Add the red wine and bring to the boil. Add the beef stock
and simmer for 2–3 minutes.

Carve the beef into 1 cm (½ in) slices. Spoon the pea and carrot purées onto two
plates. Top with a few slices of beef, spoon on the red wine sauce and serve.

Serves 2

RIB OF BEEF WITH RED WINE SAUCE

Côte de boeuf à la Bordelaise

From the Bordeaux/Southwest Region by Philippe Mouchel

❖

It's a matter of taste, but for many people there are no better red wines
in the world than the fine wines of Bordeaux in the southwest of France.
This dish of beef ribs with red wine sauce is a perfect match for the Bordeaux wines.
It's lovely served with sautéed mushrooms.

2 tablespoons vegetable oil
2 x 400 g (14 oz) beef ribs, each
    about 5 cm (2 in) thick
sea salt
freshly cracked black pepper
55 g (2 oz) butter
2 French shallots, chopped

100 ml (3½ fl oz) Bordeaux
    (or another red wine)
125 ml (4 fl oz/½ cup) rich
    veal or beef stock
a few sprigs parsley
85 g (3 oz) bone marrow

Heat the oil in a heavy frying pan and cook the beef ribs on one side for
4–5 minutes. Season with salt and pepper, turn and cook for 4–5 minutes on
the other side, adding 1 tablespoon of butter to the pan and basting the meat
from time to time. Transfer the cooked beef ribs to a dish, cover with foil and
leave to rest in a warm place.

Tip out any excess fat from the frying pan then add another tablespoon of
butter. Add the shallots and stir over medium heat for a few minutes. Add the
wine and boil for a few minutes until reduced by at least half. Add the stock and
simmer for 5 minutes. Whisk in the remaining butter and add the parsley.

Meanwhile, put the bone marrow in a small saucepan of cold salted water
and bring to a simmer. Poach over low heat for 5 minutes, then drain well.

Cut each rib into slices, arrange on plates and serve with thin slices of the bone
marrow. Spoon on the red wine sauce and serve.

Serves 3

BEEF BURGUNDY

Boeuf Bourguignon
From the Burgundy Region

❧

This is one of the most famous French regional dishes. Allow enough time to cook the dish slowly and well. It's perfect for a winter dinner party as it can be prepared in advance and enjoyed with a great red wine.

800 g (1 lb 12 oz) beef cheek (or another casserole cut such as oyster blade)
1 medium brown onion, thinly sliced
2 French shallots, thinly sliced
2 cloves garlic, crushed
1 sprig thyme or a 6 cm (2½ in) sprig rosemary
300 ml (10 fl oz) red wine
3 tablespoons olive oil
salt
freshly ground black pepper
2 teaspoons butter
1 tablespoon plain (all-purpose) flour
125 g (4 oz) bacon, finely chopped
16 baby (pickling) onions
25 small mushrooms
4 tablespoons chopped parsley

The day before you cook the dish, trim the beef of excess fat and sinews and cut it into 4–6 pieces. Place in a bowl with the onion, shallots, garlic and the thyme or rosemary. Cover with wine and stir in 1 tablespoon of the olive oil.

The following day lift the meat, onion, garlic and shallot from the wine and place on a cloth to dry. Reserve the wine and herbs as well. Season the meat with salt and pepper.

Preheat the oven to 140°C (275°F).

Heat 1 tablespoon of the oil in an ovenproof saucepan or casserole dish and brown the meat on all sides. Add the butter to the pan, followed by the reserved onion, shallot and garlic, and stir well. Sprinkle on the flour and stir well. Add the reserved wine and stir well, then add the reserved herbs. Cover with a lid and cook for about 2 hours, or until the meat is tender.

Meanwhile, heat the remaining olive oil in a frying pan and sauté the bacon over medium heat for a few minutes. Remove the bacon and set aside. Add the baby onions and brown well all over. Remove the onions, set aside and cook the mushrooms in the same pan for 2 minutes.

Towards the end of the 2 hours, add the bacon, onions and mushrooms to the casserole and stir in well. Return to the oven and cook for a further 20 minutes.

Serve sprinkled with chopped parsley.

Serves 4

BEEF AND BEER STEW

Carbonnade de boeuf

From the Northern Region by Philippe Mouchel

❧

In the north of France, beer is much more popular than wine. It is often used in cooking, as in this flavoursome winter beef casserole. It is traditional to serve this stew with large croutons spread with mustard.

3 tablespoons vegetable oil
55 g (2 oz) butter
4 beef cheeks or 1 kg (2 lb 3 oz) oyster blade steak, trimmed of excess fat and sinews
3 large onions, thinly sliced
2 teaspoons brown sugar
2 tablespoons red wine vinegar
40 g (1½ oz) plain (all-purpose) flour

750 ml (25½ fl oz/3 cups) beer (dark beer is often used in France)
250 ml (8½ fl oz/1 cup) beef stock
salt
freshly ground black pepper
a pinch of nutmeg
2 sprigs thyme
a few sprigs parsley
1 bay leaf
3 tablespoons chopped parsley
12 baby carrots

Preheat the oven to 140°C (275°F).

Heat half the oil and half the butter in a cast-iron saucepan or casserole dish and brown the beef on all sides. Transfer the beef to a plate.

Add the remaining oil and butter to the pan and cook the onions over medium heat for about 10 minutes, or until they are soft and lightly browned. Sprinkle in the brown sugar and add the vinegar. Stir in the flour and cook for a few minutes. Add the beer, stock, salt, pepper and nutmeg.

Use kitchen string to tie the thyme, parsley and bay leaf together to make a bouquet garni. Add to the pan with the meat and bring to a simmer. Skim the surface then transfer to the oven for 3 hours, or until the meat is very tender.

Remove the casserole from the oven and add the baby carrots. Cook on top of the stove for 10–12 minutes, or until the carrots are tender. Sprinkle with chopped parsley and serve.

Serves 4

GRILLED LOIN OF LAMB WITH RATATOUILLE AND TAPENADE

Agneau grillé avec ratatouille et tapenade

From the Provence Region

❧

This superb lamb dish is a perfect example of the flavoursome cuisine of Provence. The ratatouille is also wonderful served on its own.

4 loins of lamb, each about
   12 cm (5 in) long
2 tablespoons olive oil,
   plus extra for drizzling
freshly ground black pepper
1 clove garlic, finely chopped
2 tablespoons rosemary leaves,
   finely chopped
salt

Ratatouille
3 tablespoons olive oil
½ brown onion, finely diced

2 sprigs thyme, chopped
1 clove garlic, finely chopped
1 small red capsicum (pepper), diced
1 small zucchini (courgette), diced
1 small eggplant (aubergine), diced
3 tomatoes, diced

Tapenade
100 g (3½ oz) pitted black olives
3 anchovies
1 tablespoon capers
2 tablespoons olive oil

To make the ratatouille, heat the oil in a saucepan over medium heat. Add the onion and thyme and fry for a few minutes. Stir in the garlic, then add the capsicum and stir for a few minutes. Add the zucchini, eggplant and tomatoes, bring to a simmer and cook over low heat for 20–30 minutes until the vegetables are soft. Refrigerate until required. It may be reheated as you need it.

To make the tapenade, blend all ingredients to a paste. Store in the refrigerator until 10 minutes before serving.

Season the lamb loins with oil, pepper, garlic and rosemary, then marinate in the refrigerator for at least 30 minutes. Grill the lamb for 3–4 minutes on each side. Turn off the heat, cover the meat and leave it to rest for at 5 minutes before slicing.

Serve the lamb loins on a bed of hot ratatouille. Season with salt and top each loin with a tablespoon of tapenade. Drizzle with the extra olive oil and serve.

Serves 4

ROAST LAMB WITH TARBAIS BEANS

Rôti d'agneau aux haricots Tarbais

From the Gascogne-Pyrénées Region by Philippe Mouchel

❖

The cuisine north of the Pyrénées, around the city of Tarbes, is known as one of the most rustic in France and its tasty bean dishes are on offer on many restaurant menus as well as being very popular at home. If you are unable to find Tarbais beans, then use other dried beans of your choice, such as borlotti or cannellini. They need to be soaked for 24 hours in cold water.

Tarbais Beans
85 g (3 oz) dried beans of
    your choice (Tarbais, borlotti,
    cannellini), soaked for 24 hours
    in cold water
1 small carrot, chopped
1 stalk celery, chopped
½ onion, left whole
1 clove garlic
1 sprig thyme
½ bay leaf
4–5 peppercorns

1 x 6–8 cutlet lamb rack
salt
freshly ground black pepper
a little olive oil
2 cloves garlic
4 sprigs thyme, plus extra to garnish
20 g (¾ oz) butter
2 French shallots, finely chopped
½ tablespoon chopped thyme
2 teaspoons red wine vinegar
2 tablespoons chopped parsley

To prepare the Tarbais beans, drain the soaked beans and place them in a saucepan with plenty of cold water. Add the carrot, celery, onion, whole clove garlic, thyme, bay leaf and peppercorns. Bring to a simmer and cook over low heat for about 1½ hours, or until the beans are tender.

Preheat the oven to 180°C (350°F).

Season the lamb with salt and pepper. Heat a little oil in a roasting tin. Add the lamb rack and top with the whole garlic cloves and thyme sprigs. Roast the lamb for about 5 minutes, then turn it over and roast the other side for 5 minutes. Remove from the oven and leave to rest for 5 minutes in a warm place.

Meanwhile, drain the beans and remove the vegetables and herbs. Heat the butter in a saucepan. Add the shallots and chopped thyme and stir for 1 minute.

Add the beans and heat through well. Stir in the red wine vinegar and parsley and season to taste.

When ready to serve, slice the lamb rack in half. Divide the beans between two plates and top with the lamb. Garnish with sprigs of thyme and drizzle a little olive oil over the top.

Serves 2

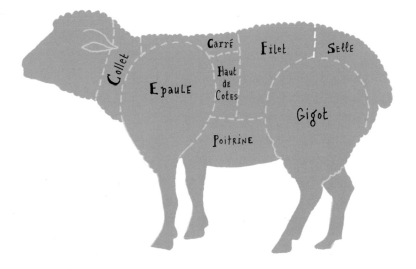

LAMB CASSEROLE WITH GREEN OLIVES

Ragoût de mouton aux olives vertes

From the Languedoc/Pyrénées Region by Philippe Mouchel

❧

The Pyrénées region is famous for its tasty lamb, and this delicious casserole benefits from being cooked for a long time at a moderate temperature. When it's ready, the meat should be soft and tender.

800 g–1 kg (about 2 lb) deboned lamb shoulder, trimmed of excess fat and cut into large cubes

salt

freshly ground black pepper

2 tablespoons olive oil, plus extra for drizzling

1 teaspoon butter

½ medium carrot, diced

½ medium onion, diced

½ tablespoon tomato paste (concentrated purée)

150 ml (5 fl oz) dry white wine

3 cloves garlic, crushed

3 x 5 cm (2 in) strips orange zest

15 green olives

300 ml (10 fl oz) chicken stock

1 large tomato, cut into 8

1 sprig thyme

1 bay leaf

a few basil leaves to garnish

Preheat the oven to 140°C (275°F).

Season the lamb with salt and pepper. Heat the oil in an ovenproof saucepan or casserole dish and brown the lamb on all sides over high heat.

Add the butter, followed by the carrot and onion, and stir for 2 minutes. Add the tomato paste and stir well. Add the wine and bring to the boil. Add the garlic, orange zest, olives, chicken stock, tomato, thyme and bay leaf. Stir well and bring to a simmer. Cover with a lid and bake in the oven for about 3 hours, or until the meat is tender.

Garnish with basil leaves, drizzle with extra olive oil and serve.

Serves 4

SLOW-COOKED LEG OF LAMB

Gigot de sept heures

From the Pyrénées Region by Philippe Mouchel

This specialty of the Pyrénées region translates as 'seven-hour lamb'. You can cook it in a little less time at a higher temperature, but it won't be quite as succulent.

1 x 1.5 kg (3 lb 5 oz) leg of lamb, trimmed of most visible fat
2 cloves garlic, cut into slivers
a little olive oil
2 sprigs thyme
a few sprigs parsley
1 bay leaf
sea salt
freshly ground black pepper
3 litres (101 fl oz/12 cups) water or beef stock
3 carrots, cut into 2 cm (¾ in) slices
2 small turnips, quartered
2 leeks, washed and cut into 2 cm (¾ in) pieces
1 onion, sliced
3 stalks celery, cut into 2 cm (¾ in) pieces
8 cloves garlic, chopped

Preheat the oven to 100–120°C (200–235°F).

Stud the lamb with the garlic slivers and tie with string. Heat the oil in a cast-iron casserole dish and brown the lamb all over.

Use kitchen string to tie the thyme, parsley and bay leaf together. Add to the casserole dish and season the lamb with a little salt and pepper. Add the water or stock and bring to a simmer on top of the stove. Cover with a lid, then transfer to the oven for 5–6 hours. Turn the lamb over in the casserole after 1 hour. During the cooking, the liquid may simmer very gently, but must not boil.

After 5–6 hours, tuck the carrots, turnips, leeks, onion, celery and garlic around the meat and cook for another hour.

Remove the casserole from the oven and transfer the meat and vegetables to a warm serving platter. Discard the bouquet garni and cover the platter with foil. On top of the stove, reduce the remaining juices to about 500 ml (17 fl oz/2 cups).

When ready to serve, remove the string from the lamb. Pour sauce over the meat and vegetables and season with a little salt and pepper before carving at the table.

Serves 8

ALSATIAN SAUERKRAUT

La choucroûte Alsacienne

From the Alsace Region by Philippe Mouchel

❦

Alsatian sauerkraut is one of the best-known French regional dishes. It's served in most Alsatian restaurants but also in many of the popular brasseries of Paris. It's often enjoyed with a glass of beer or Alsatian riesling. Sauerkraut, which literally means 'sour cabbage', is available at German-style delis and butchers, as are the pork cuts.

1 kg (2 lb 3 oz) sauerkraut
20 g (¾ oz) butter
1 large brown onion, sliced
2 bay leaves
3 cloves
12 juniper berries
600 g (1 lb 5 oz) kassler
  (smoked and salted pork
  loin), cut into 6 slices

6 x 1 cm (½ in) slices jagdwurst
  (or use strassburg or Polish sausage)
6 x 1 cm (½ in) slices kaiserfleisch
  (smoked pork belly)
375 ml (12½ fl oz/1½ cups) dry white
  wine, preferably Alsatian riesling
6 medium potatoes
6 thin Viennese sausages
3 tablespoons chopped parsley

Rinse the sauerkraut in cold water and squeeze out the excess moisture. This removes some of the sour flavour.

Melt the butter in a wide saucepan and gently fry the onion for 3 minutes. Sprinkle on half the sauerkraut and add the bay leaves, cloves and 6 of the juniper berries. Arrange the slices of kassler, jagdwurst and kaiserfleisch on top then add the remaining sauerkraut and juniper berries. Pour on the wine, cover the pan tightly and simmer over low heat for about 2 hours. This dish can also be cooked in a 150°C (300°F) oven for 2 hours.

Half an hour before serving, boil the potatoes in lightly salted water until tender. Cook the sausages in simmering water for about 10 minutes.

Spoon the cabbage onto a large platter. Arrange the cooked meats and sausages on top and surround with the potatoes. Sprinkle with parsley and serve at the table with mustard or your favourite condiments.

Serves 6

BEAN STEW WITH TOULOUSE SAUSAGES

Cassoulet Toulousain

From the Languedoc/Gascogne Region by Stéphane Langlois

❧

*Every corner of southwest France has a different version of cassoulet.
Around the town of Toulouse it's the local thick sausage that is the highlight
of this popular French classic. Confit duck and duck fat are both available
from specialist butchers and good delicatessens.*

2 tablespoons duck fat
400 g (14 oz) salted pork belly
    or shoulder, cut into 6 pieces
1 onion, diced
3 cloves garlic, crushed
1 carrot, sliced
2–3 sprigs thyme,
    finely chopped
1 stalk celery, diced
3 tablespoons plain
    (all-purpose) flour
150 ml (5 fl oz) dry white wine

1 litre (34 fl oz/4 cups) chicken stock
750 g (1 lb 10 oz) dried
    cannellini beans, soaked
    overnight in cold water
3 tablespoons tomato paste
    (concentrated purée)
salt
freshly ground pepper
6 Toulouse sausages or
    good-quality pork sausages
6 confit duck legs
3 tablespoons chopped parsley

Melt the duck fat in a cast-iron saucepan or casserole dish. Add the pieces to
the pan and brown for a few minutes. Stir in the onion and garlic, then the
carrot and thyme, and stir again. Add the celery, sprinkle on the flour and stir
for 30 seconds. Stir in the wine, then the stock. Add the beans, tomato paste,
salt and pepper and bring to a simmer. Cover the pan and cook for about 1 hour
over low heat, or until the beans are almost cooked.

Add the sausages and simmer for a further 15 minutes. Add the duck legs and
simmer gently for another 10 minutes. To serve, spoon the beans and sauce into
6 deep soup plates. Top with a piece of pork, a duck leg and a sausage, sprinkle
with chopped parsley and serve.

Serves 6

APRICOT COMPOTE WITH ALMONDS AND ARMAGNAC WITH A EWE'S MILK YOGHURT

Compote d'abricots à l'Armagnac et aux amandes avec un yaourt de brebis
From the North Pyrénées Region

❖

Using seasonal fruits, this simple French dessert is easy to prepare, and the ewe's milk yoghurt is a little more exotic than regular yoghurt. You can replace the Armagnac with another liqueur if you wish, or omit it altogether.

juice of 1 orange
juice of 1 lemon
115 g (4 oz/½ cup) caster
(superfine) sugar, plus
  2 tablespoons extra
⅓ vanilla pod, split lengthwise
12 ripe apricots,
  halved and stoned

2 tablespoons Armagnac
500 g (1 lb 2 oz) sheep's milk
  yoghurt
100 ml (3½ fl oz) pouring
  cream
20 blanched almonds, toasted

Combine the orange and lemon juice in a saucepan with the sugar and vanilla pod. Bring to a simmer. Add the apricots and return to a simmer. Cover the pan and cook the apricots over low heat until soft. Transfer the apricots and syrup to a bowl, stir in the Armagnac and leave to cool. Refrigerate until 10 minutes before serving.

Whip the yoghurt with the cream and extra sugar until smooth.

When ready to serve, add the almonds to the apricots. Spoon a little yoghurt onto four serving plates. Top with the apricots and almonds and spoon on the syrup.

Serves 4

PEACHES POACHED IN SWEET WINE

Pêches poêlées au vin doux

From the Languedoc/Provence Regions by Michael Gaté

❧

These peaches poached in sweet wine make a superb finish to a summer dinner party.
Make sure the peaches are very sweet and just ripe when you buy them.

4 just-ripe peaches, washed
30 g (1 oz) butter
4 tablespoons sugar
100 ml (3½ fl oz) Muscat de
   Rivesaltes or another sweet
   white wine
200 g (7 oz) raspberries

2 tablespoons chopped,
   peeled pistachios
icing (confectioners') sugar
   for dusting
whipped cream or ice
   cream, to serve

Three-quarters fill a medium saucepan with water and bring to the boil. Gently drop in the peaches and simmer for 2 minutes. Drain the peaches and put them in a bowl of cold water to cool. When cold, carefully peel the peaches. Cut them in half and remove the stones.

Melt the butter in a frying pan large enough to hold all the peaches. Add the sugar and stir briefly with a wooden spoon. When the sugar starts to brown, add the peach halves. Cook for 1–2 minutes then turn the peaches and shake the pan well. Add the muscat and bring to a simmer. Cover the pan with foil and cook for a few minutes until the peaches are cooked through.

To serve, place two peach halves on each plate. Garnish with raspberries and spoon on a little wine sauce. Sprinkle with pistachios and dust with icing sugar. If you wish, serve with whipped cream or ice cream.

Serves 2

POACHED PEACH AND CHERRY COUPE IN A LEMON SYRUP

Coupe de pêches et de cerises au citron
From the Languedoc Region

❖

You can find this type of luscious, fruity dessert in the Languedoc region around the stunning city of Albi, the birthplace of French painter Toulouse-Lautrec.

juice of 4 lemons
220 g (8 oz/1 cup) sugar
½ vanilla pod,
    split lengthwise
6 peaches, washed and stoned
500 g (1 lb 2 oz) cherries, pitted

200 ml (7 fl oz) whipping cream
2 tablespoons full-cream milk
2 tablespoons sugar
sweet biscuits (such as waffles,
cats' tongues, sponge fingers)

Combine the lemon juice, sugar and vanilla pod in a medium saucepan. Bring to a boil and cook for 30 seconds.

Cut each peach into 6–8 slices, but do not peel. Place in the simmering syrup and poach for 5–8 minutes. Use a slotted spoon to transfer the peach segments to a large bowl.

Return the syrup to a simmer and add the cherries. Stir gently then turn off the heat. The syrup must not boil. Pour the cherries and syrup over the peaches. Shake the bowl well then leave to cool. Once cold, refrigerate until 10 minutes before serving.

Whip the cream and milk together until light and firm, but not too stiff. Mix in the sugar.

Spoon the sweet cream into a piping bag fitted with a small serrated nozzle. Pipe a little cream into six serving glasses and top with a few peach segments and cherries. Top with a little more piped cream and finish with fruit. Serve straight away with your choice of sweet biscuits.

Serves 6

PEACH MELBA

Pêche Melba

From the Provence Region

❧

*Pêche Melba, one of the best-known French desserts, was created in 1892
by the super-talented Provençal chef Auguste Escoffier in honour of
Dame Nellie Melba, the Australian opera diva.*

1.5 litres (51 fl oz/6 cups) water
440 g (15½ oz/2 cups) sugar
½ vanilla pod, split lengthwise
thinly peeled zest of
   about ⅔ of a lemon
6 just-ripe peaches, washed
1 litre (34 fl oz/4 cups) good-
   quality vanilla ice cream
45 g (1½ oz) flaked almonds, toasted
a little icing (confectioners') sugar
   for dusting

Raspberry Sauce

300 g (10 oz) raspberries, fresh
   or frozen
juice of 1 lemon
juice of 1 orange
3 tablespoons caster
   (superfine) sugar

Combine the water, sugar, vanilla and lemon zest in a saucepan large enough to hold the peaches. Bring to a simmer and cook for 5 minutes.

Gently drop the peaches into the syrup. Bring to a slow simmer and poach the peaches for 10 minutes, until just tender. Transfer the peaches and syrup to a bowl and leave to cool. Once cold, refrigerate until 10 minutes before serving.

To make the raspberry sauce, blend all the ingredients to a purée. Strain through a fine sieve and refrigerate until ready to use.

When ready to serve, lift the peaches out of the syrup and peel them carefully. Place six scoops of ice cream in a deep serving dish. Gently place the peeled peaches on top and spoon the raspberry sauce over. Sprinkle with toasted flaked almonds, dust with icing sugar and serve immediately. Alternatively, serve the Pêche Melba in individual bowls.

Serves 6

RASPBERRY TRIFLES

Verrine aux framboises
From the Loire Valley Region

❧

The Loire Valley is known as the garden of France and red fruits are a specialty. The climate is so pleasant that the kings of France and their entourage chose to spend their summer holidays there. They built many stunning châteaux that are now the pride of the region.

Custard
250 ml (8½ fl oz/1 cup) milk
½ vanilla pod, split lengthwise
2 egg yolks
55 g (2 oz) caster (superfine) sugar
25 g (1 oz) plain (all-purpose) flour, sifted
2 oranges
2 tablespoons cointreau

300 ml (10 fl oz) whipped cream
6 savoiardi (lady fingers), cut in half
600 g (1 lb 5 oz) raspberries
a little icing (confectioners') sugar

To make the custard, heat the milk and vanilla pod in a saucepan.

In a bowl, whisk the egg yolks with the caster sugar until well combined. Gently stir in the flour. Pour on the hot milk and whisk well until smooth. Return the mixture to the rinsed-out saucepan and cook over medium heat, whisking constantly, until it begins to thicken. Tip into a bowl, whisk briefly and leave to cool. When cold, cover with plastic wrap and refrigerate.

Use a serrated knife to slice all the skin and pith from the oranges. Cut the oranges into 5 mm (¼ in) slices and lay them in a bowl. Drizzle with cointreau.

Fold the whipped cream into the cold custard, then spoon into a piping bag without a nozzle. Pipe a little custard cream into six serving glasses. Top with a piece of savoiardi, then with two slices of orange and a few raspberries. Pipe on a little more custard cream and finish with another savoiardi and a few more raspberries. Dust with icing sugar and serve.

Serves 6

SUMMER FRUIT MOUSSE

Mousse de fruits d'été

From the Loire Valley Region

❧

This is a lovely, delicate dinner party dessert. You will need to have some cooking experience and know how to use a sugar (candy) thermometer. For a beautiful presentation, you will also need four 10 cm (4 in) PVC rings.

juice of 1 lemon
juice of ½ orange
150 g (5½ oz) raspberries
⅓ vanilla pod, split open
2 leaves gelatine
100 g (3½ oz) caster
   (superfine) sugar
2 tablespoons cold water
2 egg whites

a pinch of cream of tartar
120 ml (4 fl oz) whipped
   cream
100 g (3½ oz) each
   raspberries, blackberries
   and strawberries, to serve
icing (confectioners') sugar,
   for dusting

Combine the juices, raspberries and vanilla pod in a small saucepan and bring to the boil. Boil for 5 minutes then strain through a fine sieve into a bowl. Set aside.

Soak the gelatine in a bowl of cold water for 5–10 minutes. Squeeze to remove excess water then stir into the raspberry mixture to dissolve. Set aside to cool.

Combine the sugar and water in a saucepan and bring to a simmer. Place a sugar (candy) thermometer in the pan and cook until the syrup reaches nearly 120°C (235°F). Just before the syrup reaches temperature, combine the egg whites and cream of tartar in an electric mixer and whisk to stiff peaks. With the motor running, slowly drizzle in the hot syrup. Continue whisking at a low speed for about 8 minutes, or until cool. Use a large spoon to carefully fold in the cold raspberry mixture, then the whipped cream.

Arrange the PVC rings on dessert plates. Spoon the mousse mixture into the rings, smooth the surface and refrigerate for at least 2 hours to set.

To serve, carefully run a knife blade around the inside of the rings. Top each mousse with a mixture of the berries and dust with icing sugar. Carefully lift the rings away. It looks spectacular!

Serves 4

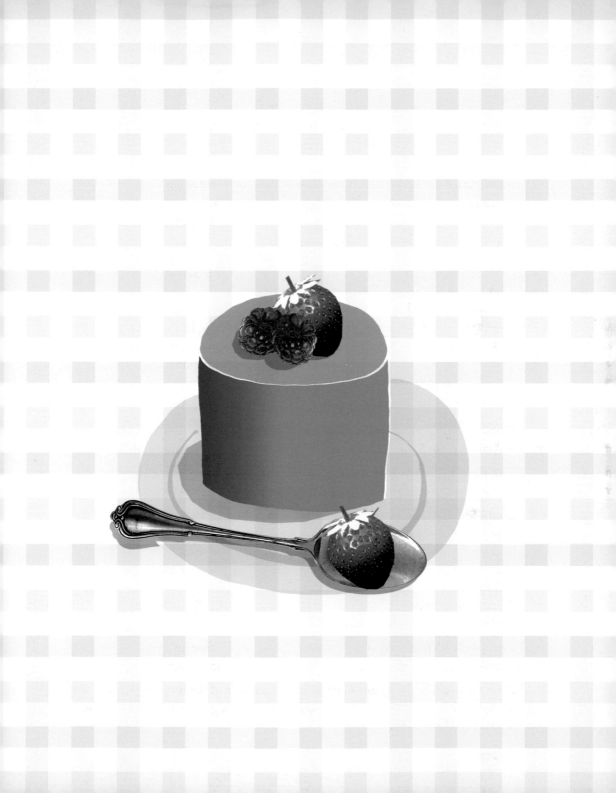

COGNAC AND GLACÉ FRUIT ICE CREAM

Glace plombières au cognac

From the Southwest Region around Cognac

❧

One of my favourite tools in the kitchen is my ice cream maker, which allows me to prepare this dessert that is to die for. Once the ice cream is made, the dessert is frozen in a chilled mould (I like to use an attractive cake or jelly mould) and it looks spectacular when it is turned out. It can be made up to three days ahead of time.

110 g (4 oz) mixed glacé
  (candied) fruit, diced
2 tablespoons cognac
500 ml (17 fl oz/2 cups) milk
¼ vanilla bean, split lengthwise
55 g (2 oz/½ cup) ground almonds
4 egg yolks

150 g (5½ oz) caster
  (superfine) sugar
250 ml (8½ fl oz/1 cup)
  whipped cream
1 kg (2 lb 3 oz) mixed summer
  berries

Place the glacé fruits in a bowl with the cognac and macerate for at least 20 minutes, or overnight if you wish.

Gently heat the milk, vanilla bean and ground almonds in a large saucepan.

Put the egg yolks and sugar in the bowl of an electric mixer and beat for about 5 minutes or until pale and creamy. Pour on the warm milk, whisking well. Return the mixture to the rinsed-out saucepan. Cook over medium heat, stirring in a figure-eight motion with a wooden spoon. Once the mixture thickens to coat the back of the spoon, remove the pan from the heat. Strain through a fine sieve and discard the almond meal. Whisk the custard briefly and leave to cool.

Tip the custard into an ice cream machine and churn according to the manufacturer's instructions. When the ice cream is quite firm, add the macerated fruits and churn briefly. Add the whipped cream and churn again until well incorporated. Transfer the ice cream to a pre-chilled 2 litre (68 fl oz/8 cup) mould and place in the freezer for at least 2 hours before serving.

When ready to serve, briefly dip the mould in warm water to loosen the ice cream, then invert it onto a deep serving platter. Cut into slices and serve with seasonal berries of your choice.

Serves 6–8

NOUGAT ICE CREAM WITH RASPBERRY SAUCE

Nougat glacé avec un coulis de framboises
From the North Provence Region

❖

This is one of my favourite desserts, but it does require some cooking experience as you need to make a caramel and use a sugar (candy) thermometer.

70 g (2½ oz) caster (superfine) sugar
1 tablespoon water
125 g (4 oz) hazelnuts, toasted
  and skinned
55 g (2 oz) honey
30 g (1 oz) liquid glucose
3 egg whites
a pinch of cream of tartar
150 g (5½ oz) glacé (candied)
  apricots, cut into 1 cm (½ in) squares

30 g (1 oz) glacé (candied)
  cherries, cut into 5 mm
  (¼ in) squares
300 ml (10 fl oz) whipped
  cream
Raspberry Sauce
  (page 100), to serve

Combine 40 g (1½ oz) of the sugar with the water in a small saucepan and cook over medium heat until it darkens to a caramel. Add the hazelnuts and stir for 2 minutes to coat them with the caramel. Very carefully tip the caramelised nuts onto a piece of lightly oiled baking (parchment) paper and spread them out. When cold, roughly chop three-quarters of the caramelised nuts. Reserve the remaining whole nuts to garnish.

Combine the honey, liquid glucose and remaining sugar in a small saucepan over medium heat. Place a sugar (candy) thermometer in the pan and cook until the syrup reaches 100°C (200°F).

Once the syrup reaches temperature, combine the egg whites and cream of tartar in an electric mixer and whisk to stiff peaks.

Continue cooking the syrup until it reaches 120°C (235°F) then slowly drizzle it onto the egg whites, whisking continuously. Continue whisking at a low speed for about 10 minutes. Transfer the ice cream mixture to the refrigerator for 10 minutes to cool.

Carefully fold the chopped hazelnuts and glacé fruits into the cooled ice cream mixture. Fold in the whipped cream then tip into a 22 cm (8½ in) cake tin lined with plastic wrap. Cover the surface with plastic wrap and freeze for at least 6 hours.

When ready to serve, dip the mould briefly in warm water to loosen the ice cream, then invert it onto a serving dish. Peel away the plastic wrap and cut into slices. Top with caramelised nuts and serve with the raspberry sauce.

Serves 8–10

CHOCOLATE CONCORDE CAKE

Gâteau concorde au chocolat

From the Paris Region by Pierrick Boyer

❧

This delicate cake was named after the Place de la Concorde in Paris.

9 egg whites

220 g (8 oz) caster (superfine) sugar

40 g (1½ oz) Dutch (unsweetended) cocoa, plus extra for dusting

150 g (5½ oz) icing (confectioners') sugar, plus extra for dusting

200 g (7 oz) dark (plain) chocolate, broken into small pieces

200 g (7 oz) unsalted butter, cut into pieces

Preheat the oven to 90°C (190°F). Line a baking tray with baking (parchment) paper and draw two 18 cm (7 in) circles on the paper.

Place 5 of the egg whites in the bowl of an electric mixer and whisk to medium-stiff peaks. Gradually whisk in 125 g (4 oz) of the caster sugar until well incorporated.

Mix the cocoa with the icing sugar and gently fold into the meringue mixture. Spoon into a piping bag fitted with a 1 cm (½ in) round nozzle. Pipe two 18 cm (7 in) spiral discs onto the prepared baking tray. Also pipe four 30 cm (12 in) long, thin 'sticks' of meringue. Bake for about 1 hour, then turn off the oven and leave the meringue for a further 30 minutes. Remove from the oven and leave to cool completely.

Place the chocolate and butter in a bowl set over a saucepan of medium-hot water. Stir together until smooth and well mixed. Set the bowl aside.

Meanwhile, whisk the remaining 4 egg whites to stiff peaks, then gradually whisk in the remaining caster sugar until well incorporated. Fold a little of the mixture into the melted chocolate, then gently fold in the remaining egg whites until just mixed. Spoon into a piping bag.

When ready to assemble, place a cake ring 18 cm (7 in) in diameter and 8 cm (3 in) high on a wire rack. Place one of the chocolate meringue discs inside, trimming the edges to fit, if necessary. Pipe a 5 cm (2 in) layer of chocolate mousse on top of the meringue, then place the second chocolate meringue disc on top. Spread the top and side of the cake with a thin layer of chocolate mousse then transfer to the freezer for about 20 minutes to set.

Transfer the cake to a serving plate and carefully lift away the cake ring. Break the thin meringue sticks into 3–4 cm pieces and stick them all over the sides and top of the cake. Take your time. The effect is stunning. Dust with a little icing sugar and cocoa powder.

Serves 8

RASPBERRY ICE CREAM CAKE WITH MERINGUE

Vacherin aux framboises

From the Alsace Region

❧

The region of Alsace is famous for this ice cream dessert, which combines fruit sorbet, vanilla ice cream, home-made meringues and whipped cream. It's one of my favourite desserts after a special dinner.
To assemble the vacherin, you will need a 2 litre (68 fl oz/8 cup) charlotte mould that should be well chilled in the freezer. Once the mould is filled, transfer to the freezer for a minimum of 1 hour before serving, so that it sets very firm.

Raspberry Sorbet
500 g (1 lb 2 oz) raspberries
300 g (10½ oz) sugar
juice of 1 lemon
juice of 2 oranges

Meringues
whites of three large eggs
a pinch of cream of tartar
120 g (4 oz) caster (superfine)
  sugar
50 g (1¾ oz) pure icing
  (confectioners') sugar, sifted

1 litre (34 fl oz/4 cups) good-
  quality vanilla ice cream
300 ml (10 fl oz) whipped
  cream
300 g (10½ oz) raspberries

To make the raspberry sorbet, combine the raspberries, sugar, lemon and orange juice in a food processor and blend to a purée. Strain through a fine sieve, then transfer to an ice cream machine and churn according to the manufacturer's instructions. When the sorbet is ready, transfer it to a pre-chilled container and place in the freezer.

If you don't have an ice cream maker, freeze the mixture in a stainless-steel bowl. When it starts to freeze, whisk for 10–15 seconds and return to freezer. Repeat at regular intervals until it becomes too firm to whisk. The whisking lightens the sorbet and prevents large ice crystals from forming.

To make the meringues, preheat the oven to 140°C (275°F). Line a baking tray with baking (parchment) paper.

Place the egg whites and cream of tartar in the bowl of an electric mixer and whisk to soft peaks. Gradually whisk in half of the caster sugar until the meringue becomes shiny and stiffer. Whisk in the remaining caster sugar and the icing sugar until well incorporated.

Spoon 12 oval spoonfuls of meringue on the baking tray, leaving a little space between them. Don't worry if the shapes are not perfect, and avoid fiddling with them. Cook for 20 minutes, then reduce the oven temperature to 100°C (200°F) and cook for a further 60 minutes. Turn off the oven and leave the meringues in the oven for a further hour to dry completely. Store in an airtight container.

To assemble the vacherin, spoon the vanilla ice cream into a chilled charlotte mould. Smooth the surface then top with the raspberry sorbet. Freeze for at least 1 hour to set well.

To unmould the vacherin, briefly dip the mould in warm water to loosen the ice cream, then invert it onto a serving dish. Stick meringues around the sides of the ice cream using a little whipped cream to attach them. Use as many meringues as necessary. Spoon the whipped cream into a piping bag fitted with a fluted nozzle and use to pipe rosettes of whipped cream in between the meringues. Top with raspberries.

Use a sharp knife to cut the vacherin into slices, so that everyone gets a meringue.

Serves 8–10

CHESTNUT CAKE

Gâteau aux marrons

From the Languedoc Region by Sébastien Burot

❧

You find lovely layered cakes such as this in many French pâtisseries and they make wonderful desserts for special occasions. To create a great-looking cake you will need to assemble it in a cake ring that is the same size as your sponge cake. You can decorate it with chocolate curls, glacé chestnuts and even gold leaves.

Rum Syrup
125 ml (4 fl oz/½ cup) water
120 g (4 oz) caster
    (superfine) sugar
2 tablespoons rum

Cake
200 g (7 oz) unsweetened purée de
    marrons (chestnut purée, which
    is available from delicatessens)
350 g (12 oz) Crème Pâtissière
    (see page 130)
300 ml (10 fl oz) whipped cream
1 x 18 cm (7 in) plain or
    chocolate sponge cake

Chocolate Icing
80 ml (2½ fl oz/⅓ cup)
    pouring cream
3 tablespoons Rum Syrup
200 g (7 oz) dark (plain)
    chocolate, cut into
    small pieces

To make the rum syrup, combine the water and caster sugar in a saucepan. Bring to a simmer and cook for 5 minutes. Stir in the rum, allow to cool, then refrigerate until ready to use.

Beat the chestnut purée and crème pâtissière until well combined. Fold in the whipped cream.

When ready to assemble, place a cake ring on a wire rack. Cut the sponge cake horizontally into three even layers and if necessary, trim them to fit into the cake ring. Place a layer of sponge cake into the base of the cake ring. Brush with a little rum syrup then spoon half the chestnut cream on top and smooth the surface. Top with another layer of sponge cake and brush with a little more syrup. Spoon in the remaining chestnut cream. Brush one side of the remaining sponge layer with syrup and place that side on top of the cream. Transfer the cake, still on the rack, to the freezer for 30 minutes to set.

While the cake is setting, make the icing. Combine the cream and rum syrup in a saucepan and bring to the boil. Stir in the chocolate until melted. Remove from heat and leave to cool slightly, stirring from time to time to keep it smooth.

Transfer the cake onto a serving plate and carefully lift away the cake ring. Use a flat spatula to glaze the cake all over with chocolate icing. Place in the refrigerator to allow the icing to set.

Serves 8–10

STRAWBERRY SPONGE CAKE

Gâteau fraisier

From the Languedoc-Roussillon Region by Pierrick Boyer

❧

Many of the sweetest French strawberries are grown in the sunny region of Languedoc-Roussillon, and this gâteau is popular in the pâtisseries of the region and, naturellement, in the top pastry shops in Paris.

To make this exquisite cake you will need to be an experienced pastry cook and for perfect presentation you will need a few pieces of special equipment, such as a cake ring and acetate plastic. Both are available from specialist food stores.

Syrup

30 g (1 oz) caster (superfine) sugar
1½ tablespoons water

Custard Filling

3 gelatine leaves
400 ml (13½ fl oz) milk
1 vanilla pod, split lengthwise
2 eggs
50 g (1¾ oz) caster (superfine) sugar
50 g (1¾ oz) cornflour (cornstarch)
100 g (3½ oz) butter, cut into cubes
400 ml (13½ fl oz) whipped cream

Cake

1 x 22 cm (8½ in) plain sponge cake
500 g (1 lb 2 oz) medium–large strawberries, halved
a little icing (confectioners') sugar, for dusting
250 g (9 oz) marzipan
a few raspberries and/or strawberries, to serve
150 ml (5 fl oz) whipped cream, to serve

To make the syrup, combine the water and sugar in a saucepan. Bring to a simmer and cook for 2 minutes to make a syrup. Set aside to cool.

To make the custard, first soak the gelatine leaves in a bowl of cold water for 5–10 minutes.

Combine the milk and vanilla pod in a saucepan and bring almost to the boil.

In a bowl, whisk the eggs, caster sugar and cornflour until well blended. Pour on the hot milk and whisk well until smooth. Return the mixture to the rinsed-out saucepan and cook over medium heat, whisking constantly, until it thickens. Tip the mixture into a bowl, whisk briefly and leave to cool a little.

Squeeze the gelatine leaves to remove excess water then stir into the custard to dissolve. Whisk in the butter cubes until melted and smooth. Pour the custard into a tray so that it can cool quickly, but don't allow it to set firm. When the custard is cold, fold in the whipped cream. Transfer the custard to a piping bag fitted with a 1 cm (½ in) round nozzle.

When ready to assemble the cake, line the base and sides of a 22 cm (8½ in) cake ring with plastic acetate, which stops the cake sticking. Place the cake ring on a baking tray lined with baking (parchment) paper.

Cut the sponge cake horizontally to create two layers. Trim 1 cm (½ in) from the edge of each, so they are smaller than the cake ring. Place one of the sponge layers in the base of the cake ring. Pipe custard into the space between the sponge and the sides of the ring. Stick strawberry halves into the custard around the edge of the ring, with the flat edges facing outwards.

Pipe a layer of custard on top of the sponge and in between the strawberries. Use a small palette knife to spread the custard up the sides of the cake ring to the top. Arrange a layer of strawberry halves on top of the custard then sit the second layer of sponge cake on top. Brush with the flavoured sugar syrup. Finish with a layer of custard, smooth the surface and refrigerate for 2 hours to set.

Dust a work surface with a little icing sugar. Roll the marzipan out thinly and cut out a 22 cm (8½ in) circle. Lift it carefully onto the top of the set cake.

Transfer the cake to a cake stand and very carefully lift away the cake ring. Decorate the cake with a few strawberries or raspberries and dust with icing sugar. Just before serving, remove the strip of acetate from the side of the cake. Cut into slices and serve with whipped cream.

Serves 8

CHERRY MOUSSE CAKE

Charlotte aux cerises

From the Alsace/Franche Comté Region

✤

In the lovely green region of South Alsace and North Franche Comté, the sides of the road are often lined with cherry groves, and cherries feature in many local desserts, as well as being transformed into a superb cherry liqueur.
For this dessert, which is a sort of French trifle, I use a loaf (bar) tin as a mould.

Custom Filling

Custard Filling
2 gelatine leaves
500 ml (17 fl oz/2 cups) milk
½ vanilla pod,
   split lengthwise
5 egg yolks
150 g (5½ oz) caster
   (superfine) sugar

one 25 cm (10 in) square
   sponge cake, about 4 cm
   (1½ in) thick
300 ml (10 fl oz) whipped cream
600 g (1 lb 5 oz) cherries,
   pitted at the last moment
Raspberry Sauce (page 100),
   to serve (optional)

To make the custard, first soak the gelatine leaves in a bowl of cold water for 5–10 minutes.

Combine the milk and vanilla pod in a saucepan and heat until nearly boiling.

In a bowl, whisk the egg yolks with the sugar until light and creamy – it takes at least 5 minutes. Pour on the hot milk and whisk well until smooth. Return the mixture to the rinsed-out saucepan and cook over medium heat, stirring with a wooden spoon, until the custard lightly coats the back of the spoon. Strain the custard into a bowl and leave it to cool slightly.

Squeeze the gelatine leaves to remove excess water then stir into the warm custard to dissolve. Transfer to the fridge to cool for 20–30 minutes, but check to ensure the custard does not set.

Line a medium loaf (bar) tin with baking (parchment) paper. Cut the sponge cake horizontally into three layers, then cut the layers into pieces and use to line the base and sides of the tin.

Fold the whipped cream into the cold custard. Pour a little custard over the sponge pieces, to about one-third of the way up the tin. Top with the pitted cherries to almost fill the tin.

Add more custard, then tap the tin lightly to help the ingredients to settle. Add more custard to fill the tin. Cover with a layer of sponge pieces to form a lid. Carefully wrap the tin in plastic wrap and refrigerate for at least 4 hours to set.

When ready to serve, carefully remove the plastic wrap and unmould the cake. Use a very sharp knife to cut it into about 10 thick slices and serve with raspberry sauce, if you wish.

Serves 8–10

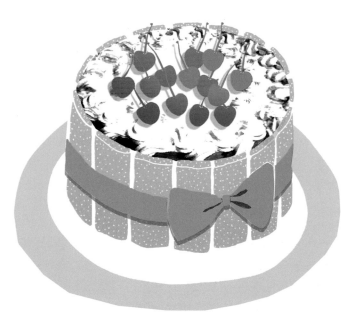

CHERRY CLAFOUTIS

Clafoutis aux cerises

From the Limousin Region by Elisabeth Kerdelhué

❧

A clafoutis is a traditional French dessert in which fresh fruit – usually cherries – are baked in a batter. It is rather like a fruit flan without the pastry. In France many people have cherry trees in their backyard – we had several at our home – and the fruit is used in desserts like this one.

700 g (1 lb 9 oz) cherries, pitted
40 g (1½ oz) plain
  (all-purpose) flour, sifted
55 g (2 oz) caster (superfine) sugar
a pinch of salt
4 eggs

600 ml (20½ fl oz)
  full-cream milk
2 egg yolks
2 tablespoons cognac or kirsch
a little icing (confectioners')
  sugar, for dusting

Preheat the oven to 180°C (350°F). Lightly butter a porcelain flan (tart) dish 28 cm (11 in) in diameter and at least 3 cm (1¼ in) deep. Arrange the cherries over the base.

Combine the flour, sugar, salt and 2 of the eggs in a bowl and mix together well. Add a little milk and mix well. Mix in the 2 remaining whole eggs and the egg yolks. Lastly, mix in the remaining milk.

Carefully strain the mixture into the dish over the cherries. Drizzle the liqueur evenly over the top. Carefully place in the oven and bake for about 45 minutes.

Remove from the oven and dust with icing sugar before serving. Take care, as it is very hot.

Serves 8

APPLE TART FLAMED WITH CALVADOS

Tarte aux pommes flambée au Calvados

From the Normandy Region by Angie Gaté

❧

*Normandy is famous for its cream, apples and a beautiful apple
liqueur called calvados, and these three special ingredients blend
together perfectly in this lovely apple tart.*

8 apples (red delicious,
  granny smith or another
  variety of your choice)
2 tablespoons water
250 g (9 oz) puff pastry
1 egg yolk
1 tablespoon water

2 tablespoons pouring
  cream
2 tablespoons caster
  (superfine) sugar
3 tablespoons calvados

Preheat the oven to 200°C (400°F). Line a baking tray with baking
(parchment) paper.

Peel 4 of the apples, then cut them into eighths and remove the cores. Cook with
the 2 tablespoons water in a covered saucepan until tender. Mash the apple to a
purée and leave to cool.

Roll out the pastry on a floured surface until it is about 30 cm (12 in) round and
about 3 mm (⅛ in) thick.

Carefully lift the pastry onto the prepared baking tray. Prick the pastry with a
fork to prevent shrinkage, then cut out a 28 cm (11 in) circle. Use the tip of a
knife blade to trace a smaller circle on the pastry, leaving a 2.5 cm (1 in) edge.
Mix the egg yolk and water together and use to brush the edge.

Spread a layer of apple purée over the centre of the pastry, leaving the edge free.
Spread the cream over the purée.

Peel, quarter and core the remaining apples and cut each quarter into four
wedges. Starting at the outer edge, arrange the apple wedges on top of the purée,
forming a spiral towards the centre. Overlap the slices a little and make sure you
leave no gaps.

Sprinkle on the sugar and bake for about 20 minutes. Reduce the oven temperature to 150°C (300°F) and bake for a further 30 minutes. The tart is cooked when the pastry is golden brown and crisp and the edges of the apples are lightly browned. The pastry base should be dry and lightly browned.

Carefully transfer the tart to a serving platter.

In a small saucepan, bring the calvados to the boil. Remove the pan from the heat and away from the stove, then carefully flame the calvados. Carefully pour the flaming liqueur over the tart and serve when the flames have subsided.

Serves 8

APPLE PIE WITH ARMAGNAC

Tarte aux pommes à l'Armagnac
From the North Pyrénées Region

⚜

*The armagnac in this pie makes a difference, but you could also use
brandy or a liqueur such as drambuie or kirsch. It's a delicious rustic
dessert and is also perfect for afternoon tea.*

4 dried figs, cut into
  1 cm (½ in) cubes
2 tablespoons armagnac
1 tablespoon finely
  grated lemon zest
20 g (¾ oz) butter
55 g (2 oz) caster
  (superfine) sugar

4 apples, peeled, cored and cut
  into 1 cm (½ in) rings
1 egg yolk
1 teaspoon water
2 x 22 cm (8½ in) squares
  rolled puff pastry
250 ml (8½ fl oz/1 cup) pouring
  cream, to serve

Place the fig pieces in a bowl with the Armagnac and lemon zest and macerate
for at least 1 hour or overnight.

Melt the butter in a large non-stick frying pan over medium heat. Add the sugar
and when it has melted, add the apple slices. Cook until the apple slices have
caramelised on one side, then turn and caramelise the other side. Add the figs
and armagnac to the pan and stir in. Remove the pan from the heat and away
from the stove, then carefully flame the mixture for a few seconds. Transfer the
fruit to a shallow dish and leave to cool.

Lightly grease a 22 cm (8½ in) loose-based flan (tart) tin. Mix the egg yolk and
water together to make eggwash.

Place the pastry squares on a floured work surface and cut out two circles to the
size of the flan tin. Lay one pastry circle in the tin and brush the edges with the
eggwash. Arrange the cold apple in the centre of the pastry, leaving an edge of
about 2.5 cm (1 in).

Carefully place the second pastry circle on top and pinch the edges together to seal. Use the tip of a knife blade to make a hole in the centre of the pastry and brush the pastry with eggwash. Make a criss-cross pattern on the pastry using the tines of a fork. Place the tart in the refrigerator for 15 minutes.

Preheat the oven to 180°C (350°F).

Bake the tart for about 30 minutes, or until the pastry is cooked and golden brown. Allow to cool slightly before carefully removing from the tin. Cut the tart into wedges and serve with cream.

Serves 8

PRUNE AND PEAR FLAN

Flan aux pruneaux et aux poires

From the Brittany Region by Pierrick Boyer

⚜

Almost every French bakery and pastry shop sells one or several varieties
of this classic tart from Brittany.

25 cm (10 in) square
   sheet puff pastry
200 g (7 oz) caster
   (superfine) sugar
40 g (1½ oz) plain
   (all-purpose) flour, sifted
4 eggs
250 ml (8½ fl oz/1 cup)
   pouring cream

250 ml (8½ fl oz/1 cup) milk
1 large or 2 small poached pears,
   cored and cut into thin slices
6 pitted prunes, cut into
   small pieces
a little icing (confectioners')
   sugar, for dusting

Preheat the oven to 180°C (350°F). Grease an 18 cm (7 in) loose-based flan
(tart) tin and arrange it on a flat baking tray.

Carefully lift the pastry onto the prepared flan tin, pushing it in gently.
Don't trim the edges as the pastry may shrink in the oven. Arrange a sheet
of baking (parchment) paper on top of the pastry and fill with rice. Bake for
10–15 minutes or until the pastry is just cooked. Remove the paper and rice.

In a bowl, mix the sugar and flour. Beat in 2 of the eggs until smooth. Beat in the
remaining 2 eggs, followed by the cream and milk to form a smooth custard.

Arrange the pears and prunes in the tart shell then carefully pour in the custard.
(Any leftover custard can be baked separately in an ovenproof porcelain dish.)
Bake for 15–20 minutes or until set and beginning to brown.

Trim the edges of the pastry. Remove the flan from the tin and transfer to a cake
stand or serving plate. Decorate with extra pears or prunes, if you wish. Dust
with icing sugar just before serving.

Serves 8

PLUM TART

Tarte aux prunes

From the Alps Region by Michael Gaté

❧

The Alpine region is famous for its wonderful fruit tarts,
prepared throughout summer and autumn with local fruits and
a dash of liqueur made from the same fruit.
The sweet shortcrust pastry is my favourite for sweet tarts and pies,
with the almonds providing a pleasant crunch. The pastry needs time to rest,
so you will need to make it at least 1 hour before using.

Sweet Shortcrust Pastry
55 g (2 oz) whole blanched
  almonds
150 g (5½ oz) unsalted butter,
  cubed
1 large egg
2 drops pure vanilla essence
a pinch of salt
100 g (3½ oz) icing
  (confectioners') sugar
250 g (9 oz/1⅔ cups) plain
  (all-purpose) flour

85 g (3 oz) sugar
85 g (3 oz) butter
1 whole egg
1 egg yolk
2 tablespoons plum liqueur
  (or use kirsch, Pear William
  or brandy)
85 g (3 oz) ground almonds
1 tablespoon plain (all-purpose)
  flour, sifted
8 large plums, halved and stoned
  (blood plums are lovely)
a little icing (confectioners') sugar,
  for dusting

To make the sweet shortcrust pastry, chop the almonds coarsely but evenly in a food processor. Add the butter, egg, vanilla and salt and process briefly until the butter has softened slightly. Continue to blend, gradually adding the icing sugar and flour until the pastry is well mixed. Tip the pastry out onto a work surface and use your hands to shape it into a ball. Wrap in plastic wrap. Flatten slightly and refrigerate for at least 1 hour before using.

Preheat the oven to 200°C (400°F). Grease a 25 cm (10 in) square or a 28 cm (11 in) round flan (tart) tin and place it on a flat baking tray.

Combine the sugar and butter in a small food processor and blend until well combined and creamy. Add the egg and egg yolk and blend. Add the liqueur, then the ground almonds and flour, and blend until combined. Transfer the almond cream to a bowl.

Remove the pastry from the fridge and knead slightly to soften. Lightly flour two 30 cm (12 in) squares of baking (parchment) paper. Place the pastry between them and roll out to a thickness of about 3 mm (⅛ in). Carefully lift the pastry into the prepared flan tin, pushing it in gently. Don't trim the edges as the pastry may shrink in the oven.

Spread the almond cream over the pastry base and up the sides. Arrange the plum halves on top, skin side down, working from the edge to the centre. Bake for 20 minutes then trim the pastry edges neatly.

Reduce the oven temperature to 150°C (300°F) and bake for a further 35–40 minutes or until the pastry base is dry and lightly browned. Just before serving, dust the tart with icing sugar.

Serves 6–8

RASPBERRY TARTLETS

Tartelettes aux framboises
From the Loire Valley Region

❧

I prepared this dessert hundreds of times during my chef's apprenticeship in the Loire Valley. The pastry shells and crème pâtissière can both be made ahead of time, but if you make the pastry on the same day, be sure to allow time for it to rest for at least an hour before rolling out. Avoid assembling the tartlets more than two hours before serving as the pastry will become soggy.

Crème Pâtissière
250 ml (8½ fl oz/1 cup) milk
2 egg yolks
⅓ vanilla pod, split lengthwise
55 g (2 oz) caster
  (superfine) sugar
30 g (1 oz) plain (all-purpose)
  flour, sifted

Sweet Shortcrust Pastry
  (page 128), chilled
3 tablespoons pouring cream
3 tablespoons apricot jam
a splash of water
600 g (1 lb 5 oz) raspberries

To make the crème pâtissière, bring the milk to a boil in a medium saucepan.

In a bowl, whisk the egg yolks, vanilla pod and sugar for 2 minutes. When well blended, whisk in the flour. Pour on the hot milk and whisk well until smooth.

Return the mixture to the rinsed-out saucepan and cook over medium heat, whisking constantly, until the mixture thickens and comes to a boil. Once it reaches a boil, tip the mixture into a bowl. Whisk briefly and leave to cool. When cold, discard the vanilla pod, cover the crème pâtissière with plastic wrap and refrigerate until ready to use.

When ready to make the tartlets, preheat the oven to 200°C (400°F). Grease twenty 6 cm (2½ in) loose-based tartlet tins and arrange them on a baking tray.

Flour a work surface. Remove the pastry from the fridge and knead lightly. Roll out the pastry to about 3 mm (⅛ in) thick and cut into squares to fit the tartlet moulds. Line the moulds with the pastry, pushing it in gently. Trim the edges with your fingertips, taking care not to make them too thin and fragile. Cook for about 10 minutes, or until the edges have browned and the pastry is cooked. Remove from the oven and leave to cool before unmoulding.

Mix the crème patissière with the cream.

Heat the apricot jam with a little water to make a runny glaze.

To assemble the tartlets, place a spoonful of pastry cream into each pastry shell and spread it a little. Arrange the raspberries decoratively over the cream, working from the edge to the centre. Brush lightly with the apricot glaze and chill until ready to serve.

Makes about twenty 6 cm (2½ in) tartlets

ET VOILA MADAME

MONT BLANC CHESTNUT CAKES

Petits gâteaux Mont Blanc

From the Alps Region by Pierrick Boyer

⚜

The French are mad about chestnuts and this dessert, using a luscious chestnut cream, was created to celebrate the beauty of the alpine Mont Blanc peak. You need special pastry equipment, in particular a piping bag fitted with a Mont Blanc nozzle.

250 g (9 oz) Sweet Shortcrust Pastry (page 128)
55 g (2 oz) ground almonds
55 g (2 oz) icing (confectioners') sugar, plus extra for dusting
55 g (2 oz) plain (all-purpose) flour, sifted
55 g (2 oz) butter, softened
1 egg
6 teaspoons orange marmalade

6 small meringues, the size of a ball of cotton wool
100 g (3½ oz) sweet chestnut cream (crème de marrons, which is available from delicatessens)
100 g (3½ oz) unsweetened chestnut purée (purée de marrons, which is available from delicatessens)
100 ml (3½ fl oz) whipped cream

Preheat the oven to 170°C (325°F). Lightly grease six 6 cm (2½ in) tartlet rings. Arrange the rings on a flat baking tray.

Roll the pastry out to a thickness of 3 mm (⅛ in). Cut out six 10 cm (4 in) discs of pastry and use to line the tartlet rings, pushing the pastry in gently. Trim the edges neatly.

In a bowl, combine the almonds, sugar, flour and butter. Add the egg and mix until smooth. Spoon into a piping bag and neatly fill the pastry cases three-quarters full. Bake for about 15 minutes or until the pastry is cooked and golden brown. Remove from the oven and leave to cool, then turn the tartlets out.

Spread 1 teaspoon of marmalade on each tartlet, and top with a small meringue.

In a bowl, combine the chestnut cream and chestnut purée. Spoon the mixture into a piping bag fitted with a special Mont Blanc nozzle and use it to pipe the traditional vermicelli-like icing over the top of the meringues to cover them well. Dust with icing sugar. Use a piping bag fitted with a star nozzle to pipe cream rosettes of 'snow' on the summit of your mini Mont Blanc cakes. Refrigerate until 10 minutes before serving.

Makes 6 little cakes

PUFF PASTRY AND ALMOND CREAM CAKE

Pithiviers

From the Loire Valley Region by Sébastien Burot

❦

This classic cake is also known as Galette des Rois and it is really popular on 6 January, when French Catholics celebrate the Epiphany – the arrival of the Three Wise Kings. The Kings' cake is usually purchased from the local pâtisserie.

Almond Cream
125 g (4 oz) butter
125 g (4 oz) caster (superfine) sugar
2 eggs
125 g (4 oz) almond meal
2 tablespoons rum
30 g (1 oz) plain (all-purpose) flour

2 x 25 cm (10 in) square sheets puff pastry (or 500 g/1 lb 2 oz) puff pastry)
1 egg yolk
2 tablespoons water

Preheat the oven to 220°C (425°F). Line a flat baking tray with baking (parchment) paper.

To make the almond cream, combine the butter and sugar in the bowl of an electric mixer and beat until well combined. Add the eggs one at a time, mixing well after each addition. Add the almond meal and mix well. Add the rum and flour and mix well. Spoon the mixture into a piping bag without a nozzle.

Lay the pastry sheets out on a work surface (or roll out to a thickness of 5 mm/¼ in). Using a large plate or similar, cut out two 25 cm (10 in) rounds.

Carefully lift one pastry round onto the prepared baking tray. Use the tip of a knife to trace a smaller circle, about 17 cm (6½ in) in diameter, on the pastry.

Mix the egg yolk and water together to make eggwash and use to brush the outer edge of the pastry. Pipe a generous mound of almond cream in the centre. Cover with the second pastry disc and press the edges together to seal. Brush with more eggwash. Use the blade of a small knife to mark the surface with curved lines that radiate from the centre to the edges in an attractive pattern.

Bake for 15 minutes, then reduce the oven temperature to 200°C (400°F) and bake for a further 20–25 minutes, or until the cake is browned underneath.

Serves 6–8

PARIS BREST GÂTEAU

From the Paris Region by Philippe Mouchel

❖

Named after a bicycle race from, you guessed it, Paris to Brest, this delicious French gâteau is made by most traditional French pâtissiers and is often available in individual portions. You can prepare both the crème pâtissière pralinée and the choux pastry rings the day before you serve the dessert.

Crème Pâtissière Pralinée
55 g (2 oz) butter, softened
55 g (2 oz) hazelnut pralinée or chocolate pralinée (or use Nutella)
Crème Pâtissière (page 130), chilled

Choux Pastry
100 ml (3½ fl oz) water
150 ml (5 fl oz) milk
½ teaspoon salt
2 teaspoons sugar
85 g (3 oz) butter, cut into small pieces

150 g (5½ oz/1 cup) plain (all-purpose) flour, sifted
4 eggs
1 egg yolk
1 teaspoon water
about 55 g (2 oz) flaked almonds
icing (confectioners') sugar, for dusting

To make the crème pâtissière pralinée, beat the butter with the hazelnut pralinée until well combined. Add the crème pâtissière and mix well to combine. Refrigerate until ready to use.

Preheat the oven to 200°C (400°F). Place a 20 cm (8 in) flan (tart) ring on a baking tray lined with baking (parchment) paper.

To make the choux pastry, combine the water, milk, salt, sugar and butter in a medium saucepan and bring to a simmer. When the butter has dissolved, lower the heat and add the flour in one go, stirring vigorously with a wooden spoon for a few minutes until it forms a smooth mass.

Transfer the mixture to the bowl of an electric mixer fitted with the K beater and mix on medium speed. Add the eggs one at a time, mixing well after each addition, until the dough is smooth. Spoon into a large piping bag fitted with a 1 cm (½ in) nozzle.

Pipe a circle of dough inside the flan ring close to the edge. Pipe a second circle inside the first one then pipe a third circle on top of these two circles.

Mix the egg yolk and water together to make eggwash and brush over the pastry. Sprinkle on the flaked almonds and bake for 20 minutes. Reduce the oven temperature to 150°C (300°F) and bake for a further 25 minutes. Turn off the oven and leave the pastry in the oven to dry for about 1 hour. Remove from the oven and leave on a wire rack until completely cold. Carefully lift away the flan ring.

When nearly ready to serve, spoon the chilled crème pâtissière pralinée into a piping bag fitted with a serrated nozzle. Split the pastry in half horizontally and fill the base to a height of about 2.5 cm (1 in). Gently place the pastry lid on top. Dust with icing sugar and serve straight away. Alternatively, store in the refrigerator until 10 minutes before serving.

Serves 8

ST HONORÉ CAKE

Gâteau St Honoré

Popular all over France by Pierrick Boyer

❖

Pierrick Boyer, our team's talented pâtissier, prepared this popular and delicious French gâteau to celebrate Bastille Day, the French national day on 14 July. It is a rather elaborate cake and to make it you will need good baking skills and some specialist equipment, such as a St Honoré nozzle.

250 ml (8½ fl oz/1 cup) water
100 g (3½ oz) butter
a pinch of salt
165 g (6 oz) plain (all-purpose) flour, sifted
5 large eggs
20 cm (8 in) square rolled puff pastry
200 g (7 oz) fondant (available from specialist food stores)

250 g (9 oz) glucose syrup
300 g (10½ oz) Crème Patissière (page 130)
300 g (10½ oz) whipped cream
a few halved strawberries
icing (confectioners') sugar, for dusting

Preheat the oven to 180°C (350°F). Line two baking trays with baking (parchment) paper.

Combine the water, butter and salt in a medium saucepan and bring to a simmer. When the butter has dissolved, lower the heat and add the flour in one go, stirring vigorously with a wooden spoon for a few minutes until it forms a smooth mass.

Transfer the mixture to the bowl of an electric mixer fitted with the K beater and mix on medium speed. Add the eggs one at a time, mixing well after each addition, until the dough is smooth. Spoon into a large piping bag fitted with a 1 cm (½ in) nozzle.

Place the puff pastry square on a floured surface and cut out a 20 cm (8 in) disc. Lift it carefully onto the prepared baking tray. Pipe a circle of choux pastry around the edge of the puff pastry disc. Now pipe a loose spiral shape, starting from the centre and working to the edge.

Pipe twelve 3 cm (1¼ in) choux puffs onto the second prepared baking tray. Place both trays in the oven and cook for about 20 minutes, until the pastries are golden brown and cooked. Remove from the oven and cool the cake and choux puffs on a wire rack.

Place the fondant and glucose syrup in a small saucepan. Bring to the boil and cook to a caramel. Very carefully dip the choux puffs into the hot caramel then place them, caramel side down, on a non-stick baking tray to cool. When cold they will have a nice smooth caramel edge.

Dip the opposite sides of the choux puffs into the caramel, then stick them onto the cake, in a circle around the edge, so the flat caramel sides are uppermost. Make sure you set one choux puff aside.

In a bowl fold together the crème pâtissière and the whipped cream and spoon into a piping bag fitted with a special St Honoré nozzle. Pipe a generous amount into the centre of the cake, forming the traditional little rounded peaks. (If you don't have a special nozzle, pipe it in as attractively as you can.)

Using a serrated knife, slice the choux puffs in half horizontally and remove the caramelised lids. Carefully fill the choux halves that are attached to the cake, then replace the lids. Place the reserved choux puff in the centre of the cake. As a final flourish, decorate the top with strawberry halves and dust with icing sugar.

Serves 8

SAVOIE SPONGE CAKE

Gâteau de Savoie
From the Alps Region

✦

*My grandmother, who inspired me to become a chef, baked one of these
lovely gâteaux each time we had a special family celebration. I love to serve it
with a runny custard and fresh fruits.*

85 g (3 oz) plain (all-purpose) flour
85 g cornflour (cornstarch)
6 eggs, separated
grated zest of 1 lemon
300 g (10½ oz) caster
   (superfine) sugar

a pinch of cream of tartar
icing (confectioners') sugar,
   for dusting

Preheat the oven to 180°C (350°F). Butter a 25 cm (10 in) round cake tin.

Sift the flours together.

Put the egg yolks, lemon zest and 150 g (5½ oz) of the caster sugar in the bowl
of an electric mixer and beat until very pale and mousse-like.

Add the cream of tartar to the egg whites and whisk them to stiff peaks.
Gradually whisk in the remaining caster sugar until well incorporated. Gently
fold the egg whites into the egg yolks. Lastly, fold in the sifted flours, being
careful not to over-mix.

Pour the cake mixture into the prepared tin and smooth the surface. Dust with
a little icing sugar and bake for 35–40 minutes. Remove from the oven and cool
for about 10 minutes on a wire rack. Turn out of the tin and cool completely
before serving.

Serves 10–12

WALNUT CAKE

Gâteau aux noix
From the Alps Region

❧

This family cake is very popular in the region of Grenoble, famous for its large production of walnuts.

Cake
165 g (6 oz) walnuts
150 g (5½ oz) butter
finely grated zest of 1 lemon
150 g (5½ oz) sugar
4 eggs, separated
75 g (2¾ oz/¾ cup) dried
   breadcrumbs
a pinch of cream of tartar

Icing
55 ml (2 fl oz) water
100 g (3½ oz) sugar
2 drops red wine vinegar
10 walnut halves
a little icing
   (confectioners') sugar,
   for dusting

Preheat the oven to 150°C (300°F). Butter a 22 cm (8½ in) cake tin, line the base with baking (parchment) paper, then butter the paper.

Place the walnuts in a food processor and grind to a coarse meal.

Using an electric mixer, beat the butter, lemon zest and half the caster sugar until pale and creamy. Add the egg yolks, one at a time, beating on medium speed. Add the breadcrumbs and chopped walnuts and mix well.

Whisk the egg whites and cream of tartar to medium-stiff peaks. Gradually whisk in the rest of the caster sugar until well incorporated. Add a third of the egg whites to the batter and fold in well. Carefully fold in the remaining whites.

Pour into the prepared cake tin and smooth the surface. Bake for 1 hour.

Remove the cake from the oven and cool for 5 minutes before turning out onto a wire rack.

To make the icing, combine the water, sugar and vinegar in a small saucepan and bring to the boil. Cook to a light brown caramel. Pour the icing slowly onto the centre of the cake and use a spatula to spread it out smoothly. Garnish with walnut halves and dust the edges of the cake with icing sugar.

Serves 8–10

KOUGELHOPF GÂTEAU

From the Alsace Region by Philippe Mouchel

❦

*This wonderful yeast cake is a great specialty of Alsace.
You can find it in every pâtisserie and bakery in the region and at the
better hotels it is usually on offer for breakfast. You will need a special
gugelhopf mould to create the traditional fluted, curved shape.*

100 g (3½ oz) raisins
55 ml (2 fl oz) rum
12 g (½ oz) fresh yeast
60 ml (2 fl oz/¼ cup) milk, boiled
  and cooled to lukewarm
250 g (9 oz/1⅔ cups) plain
  (all-purpose) flour
40 g (1½ oz) caster
  (superfine) sugar
1 teaspoon salt
4 eggs

185 g (6 oz) butter, at room
  temperature, plus extra for
  greasing
20 g (¾ oz) extra butter to butter
  the gugelhopf mould
100 g (3½ oz) flaked almonds
1 egg yolk
1 tablespoon water
icing (confectioners') sugar,
  for dusting (optional)

Put the raisins in a bowl with the rum and leave to macerate overnight.

Mix the yeast with the warm milk in a small bowl.

Combine the flour, caster sugar, salt and yeast mixture in the bowl of an electric mixer fitted with the dough hook. Beat on medium speed. Add the eggs, one at a time, beating well after each addition. Beat for about 5 minutes until the dough is smooth and elastic.

Turn the mixer speed to low and add the butter, bit by bit. Once it's all incorporated, increase the speed to medium again and beat for about 8 minutes until the dough comes away from the sides of the bowl. Briefly mix in the macerated raisins.

Transfer the dough to a bowl, cover with a clean cloth and leave to rise at room temperature for about 2 hours.

Knock back the dough by punching it lightly with your fists a few times. Roll it out to a rectangle and fold it onto itself to form a sausage shape.

Butter a gugelhopf mould with the extra butter and scatter the flaked almonds onto the sides and base. Place the dough into the mould, adjusting it gently to fit. Mix the egg yolk and water together and use to seal the ends together. Leave to rise in a warm place (about 25°C/75°F is ideal) for another 2 hours.

Preheat the oven to 200°C (400°F). Bake the gugelhopf for 20 minutes then cover with baking (parchment) paper and cook for a further 20 minutes. Remove the cake from the oven and place on a rack to cool. Turn out after about 15 minutes and leave to cool completely. Dust with icing sugar just before serving.

Serves 8–10

MACARONS

Macarons

From the Paris Region by Pierrick Boyer

❧

These delicious small, round cakes are crunchy on the outside and smooth and soft in the centre. They were made famous by the great Parisian pâtisserie Ladurée, where every year a new flavour of macaroon is created. A little experience is required to make macaroons well, so you may need to make a few batches to perfect the technique.

50 ml (1¾ fl oz) water
150 g (5½ oz) caster (superfine) sugar
120 g (4 oz) egg whites
2 vanilla pods, seeds scraped
160 g (5½ oz) ground almonds

160 g (5½ oz) icing (confectioners') sugar
160 ml (5½ fl oz) pouring cream
160 g (5½ oz) dark (plain) chocolate

Preheat the oven to 145°C (280°F). Line 2 baking trays with baking (parchment) paper.

Combine the caster sugar and water in a saucepan and bring to a simmer. Place a sugar (candy) thermometer in the pan and cook until the syrup reaches 121°C (250°F).

Just before the syrup reaches temperature, place 2 of the egg whites in an electric mixer and whisk to stiff peaks. With the motor running, slowly drizzle in the hot syrup. Continue whisking at a low speed for a few minutes.

In a mixing bowl, combine the remaining egg whites with the vanilla seeds, almonds and icing sugar. Mix in a spoonful of the beaten egg whites to loosen the mixture. Then use a plastic scraper to mix in the remaining egg whites. Transfer the mixture to a piping bag fitted with a 1 cm (½ in) nozzle.

Pipe small 3 cm (1¼ in) mounds of the mixture onto the baking trays, spacing them evenly. Tap the trays lightly on a work surface to settle the mixture. Leave to rest for 1 hour, then bake for 8–10 minutes.

Meanwhile, bring the cream to the boil. Pour the hot cream onto the chocolate and stir until very smooth. Leave the chocolate to cool and firm up a little, but don't allow it to set. Spoon into a piping bag.

Pipe neat dollops of chocolate onto the flat sides of half the macarons. Top each with a macaron and sandwich together. Store in an airtight container.

Makes 30–35

RASPBERRY FRUIT JELLIES

Pâte de fruit aux framboises

From the Limousin Region by Philippe Mouchel

❦

You find these exquisite, soft and flavoursome fruit jellies in the best French pâtisseries and they are often served with coffee in top restaurants.

Making these jellies requires some experience and you will need a few items of specialist equipment, such as a sugar (candy) thermometer and a fruit jelly frame.

1.2 kg (2 lb 10 oz) strained
   raspberry purée
1.1 kg (2 lb 7 oz) caster
   (superfine) sugar
30 g (1 oz) apple pectin
200 g (7 oz) liquid glucose

1½ tablespoon citric acid
2 tablespoons raspberry liqueur
200 g (7 oz) sugar

Line a tray with baking (parchment) paper and place a 40 cm (16 in) square fruit jelly frame on top.

Place the strained raspberry purée in a saucepan and bring to a simmer.

Mix 100 g (3½ oz) of the caster sugar with the apple pectin and stir into the raspberry purée. Add the liquid glucose and the remaining sugar and bring to a slow boil.

Place a sugar (candy) thermometer in the pan and cook until the syrup reaches 108°C (226°F). Stir from time to time and brush the side of the pan with a little water if necessary, to keep it clean.

Dissolve the citric acid in the raspberry liqueur and add it to the purée once it reaches 108°C (226°F). Very carefully pour the jelly mixture into the frame and spread it evenly. Allow to cool, then refrigerate for at least 2 hours to set.

Gently remove the frame and cut the fruit jelly into 3 cm (1¼ in) squares. Place the jellies onto a plate of sugar and coat delicately with sugar. Store in a dry cake tin in layers separated with baking (parchment) paper.

Makes about 150 jellies

ALMOND AND HONEY NOUGAT

Nougat aux amandes et au miel

From the Provence-Rhône Region

❦

Nougat is the specialty of the town of Montélimar at the northern border of Provence and this festive sweet is one of the thirteen traditional Provençal Christmas desserts.

It takes experience to make nougat as you need to be able to juggle timing and temperatures – and you must take care not to burn yourself with the hot honey and syrup. You will need a sugar (candy) thermometer to ensure the syrup and honey reach the exact temperatures. The syrup should take longer to reach 150°C (300°F) than the honey takes to reach 135°C (275°F).

450 g (1 lb) raw almonds (skins on)
100 g (3½ oz) pistachio nuts, skinned and roughly chopped
100 g (3½ oz) hazelnuts, skins removed if possible
6 sheets edible rice paper
125 ml (4 fl oz/½ cup) water

375 g (13 oz) caster (superfine) sugar
185 g (6½ oz) liquid glucose
250 g (9 oz) honey
2 large egg whites
a pinch of cream of tartar

Preheat the oven to 150°C (300°F). Line a roasting tin with baking (parchment) paper. Line a 35 x 25 x 2.5 cm (14 x 10 x 1 in) swiss roll (jelly roll) tin with baking paper.

Put all the nuts in the prepared roasting tin and dry-roast in the oven for about 20 minutes, stirring occasionally. Remove the nuts from the oven and keep warm until ready to use.

Reduce the oven temperature to 100°C (200°F).

To make a syrup, combine the water, sugar and glucose in a saucepan and bring to the boil over medium heat. Place a sugar (candy) thermometer in the pan and cook until the syrup reaches 150°C (300°F).

At the same time, heat the honey in a second saucepan. Bring to the boil over medium heat and cook to 135°C (275°F).

Just before the honey and syrup reach temperature, combine the egg whites and cream of tartar in an electric mixer and whisk to soft peaks. With the motor running, slowly drizzle in the honey. Then drizzle in the hot syrup. Continue whisking at a low speed for about 5 minutes. Fold the roasted nuts into the nougat.

Arrange 3 sheets of rice paper in the prepared tin. Tip in the nougat mixture and smooth the surface with a wet metal spoon. Lay the remaining 3 sheets of rice paper on top and leave the nougat to cool before covering with plastic wrap. Refrigerate when cold.

Remove the plastic wrap and turn the nougat out onto a chopping board. Use a large knife to cut into 2.5 cm (1 in) squares. The nougat becomes softer at room temperature.

Makes about 100 pieces

INDEX

❧

ACKNOWLEDGEMENTS

❧

I wish to express my very special thanks to SBS, particularly Les Murray and Ken Shipp, for commissioning me to produce *Taste Le Tour* over the past five years.

I want to thank my wife, Angie Gaté, who took part in all aspects of the project.

I am very grateful to Peter Warren who helped produce the series.

Most of all, thanks to the French chefs, pastry chefs, friends and family members who have contributed recipes published in this book, especially Philippe Mouchel, Sebastian Burot, Pierrick Boyer, Stéphane Langlois, Elisabeth Kerdelhué, Angie Gaté and Michael Gaté.

Lastly, thanks to Hardie Grant's publishing team for making the experience of putting the book together so enjoyable.